D0937144

PONDS

Building
Maintaining
Enjoying

The First Complete Book of
Farm Pond Management

By Carolyn Garrick Stern

Design: B.J. Johnson

Technical assistance:
Norman Latona, Southeastern Pond Management
Mary Leidner, District Conservationist, USDA-NRCS
John Leidner, *Progressive Farmer* Southeast Regional Editor

Illustrations:
Ray E. Watkins, Jr., Ralph Mark

Photographs:
Vann Cleveland, Pat Peacock, John Leidner, Geoffrey Gilbert

©1996 by Progressive Farmer, Inc.
Manufactured in the
United States of America
Library of Congress Catalog Number:
96-92550
International Standard Book Number:
0-8487-1298-6

Come on in; the water's fine

You might call them ponds, lakes, or tanks, depending on your part of the country. But however you refer to them, these water areas are important parts of the rural landscape. And you *can* have one that will reward you with pleasure and increased value to your farmstead with minimal investment in money and labor, if you plan carefully.

Maybe you've always hankered for a fishing spot of your very own or a place your family could swim and picnic. Or you need an extra water supply for livestock or irrigation. Or perhaps you just like to watch the wildlife that a waterhole draws.

This book will help you get more out of the underwater acres you have, or want to have, on your place. You'll learn the importance of site choice and pre-planning. You'll get fish stocking instructions and ways to keep fish healthy and in balance.

And, best of all, you'll discover lots of ways that a pond can add to your outdoor enjoyment.

TABLE OF CONTENTS

TABLE OF CONTENTS

Building It Right

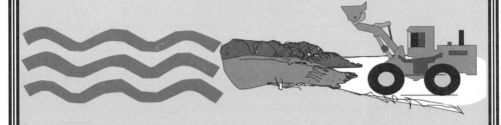

Points to Pond-er

▶ **The key is to plan, plan, plan.**

▶ **Consider the site carefully.**

▶ **Determine the soil type.**

▶ **Keep the landscape simple.**

▶ **Allow for boat storage.**

Note: Talk to the experts at your local office of the USDA Natural Resources Conservation Service before you put a shovel in the ground.

I.

BUILDING

This book is filled with suggestions on how to build a farm pond and take care of it, and, above all, how to get the most enjoyment from it.

Here you'll find basic information that will allow you to determine the best site and the most important purpose the pond will serve for you and your family.

It's not intended to give you every fact that you need in order to jump on a bulldozer and start digging. In most cases, you'll need a contractor with a local reputation for successful pond building to do that.

For complex installations, you'll also want to consult an engineer.

And you'll need information about site selection, government regulations, fish management, and other valuable tips that you can get from your state department of conservation, as well as local offices of the USDA Natural Resources Conservation Service and the U.S. Department of Wildlife and Fisheries.

But the future maintenance will fall for the most part on you. You'll find your job much simpler if you spend the time and effort up front with that contractor and those agencies after you've read over these guidelines.

Pond-building sounds simple enough: You've got to have a spot that will get enough water to keep your pond filled and a basin with the right elements to hold that water.

These criteria depend on the lay of your land, the availability of water, and the content of the soil, which we'll talk about in greater detail further on.

The size of your pond and how and where you build it also depends on its purpose. Do you want enough bass to keep your line jumping all summer? Or maybe you just like to watch the wind make waves, and your family would enjoy a place for swimming and for cookouts.

It could be that you want a pond to work for you; you've always needed a ready source of water for livestock, irrigation, or fire protection.

If your pond is built right in the beginning and maintained on a regular basis, the benefits it will add in property value and personal enjoyment will far outweigh the cost and labor involved.

Now, for the details.

PRIMARY PURPOSE

Once you begin thinking that a water spot might be a possibility, all kinds of uses will spring to your mind.

And a pond can be planned so that it will serve a variety of purposes.

However, before you decide that a pond is the answer to all your water needs, consider the compatibility of those desired activities.

Say you want a great fishing hole and family swimming spot, but you need irrigation water. The chemicals you may have to use to control aquatic weeds to allow maximum fish production may be OK for swimming but unsuitable for your crops.

Also, hot, dry weather is when you'd need the water for irrigation, and there may not be enough water to support recreation and fish as well.

Or you might like the added attraction of having wildlife visit your recreation area. But swimmers won't relish diving into a pond with the type of plants that are intended to attract wildlife.

A well-planned and maintained pond can add economic value to your acreage, in addition to giving you a spot for recreation and relaxation.

And although ducks and geese are pretty in a pond, the conditions they create won't be conducive to swimming.

However, if your pond is for fishing only, a few ducks and geese (not a whole flock) will not affect the condition of the water. And the plantings to attract other wildlife can be confined to specific areas.

A pond that's primarily a recreation spot also can provide a livestock watering facility. Since livestock make a mess of pond sides and muddy the water, you can have the best of both uses by fencing them out and adding a separate gravity-fed watering tank below the dam.

CHOOSING THE SITE

The performance of nearby ponds that have a similar profile to yours, as far as water source and soil, is a good indicator of the suitability of a proposed site.

If you have several viable spots on your land for a pond, a number of factors could point you toward the ideal place.

Siting it close to your house will make it convenient for recreation and might provide a ready source for water in case of fire or for barnyard animals.

But there are advantages to locating it in a secluded spot of woods. Wildlife will be more attracted to a pond out of sight of people, and many fishermen like that kind of isolation too.

Clean water is a must for any use. Check upstream or uphill for shops, garages, barns, or septic systems that might contribute to contamination of streams, wells, or springs. And if you'll be getting runoff from crop fields or cattle grazing areas, excess nutrients can upset fish management and encourage weed growth.

The site needs to be protected from a "public nuisance" standpoint. If the pond is readily visible and accessible from public roads, find out all you can about local laws concerning your liability in case of injury from use of the pond, whether you've given permission or not.

You may be able to make changes in siting that will allow you some protection. In any case, if the pond is near your property line, plan to install a fence on the lines.

Also check the site for buried pipelines or cables and steer away from above-ground powerlines. A fisherman could snag a wire instead of a bass.

A final consideration: To get the most out of your construction dollars, locate the pond where you can obtain the most water with the least amount of earthfill or excavation.

For example, if you dig a 1-acre pond, 3 feet deep, you will move about 4,800 cubic yards of dirt. At an estimated cost of $1.50 per cubic yard, that alone totals $7,200. Talk to neighbors who have built ponds and the local office of the NRCS for approximate costs in your area.

DAM OR DIG?

Your site will determine whether an embankment (impoundment) or excavated (dug out) pond is for you. Or your best bet may be a combination of both.

Areas with a natural valley are more suitable for embankment ponds. Although the costs for heavy equip-

ment and dam construction may be higher up front, you usually get more water for the dollar spent. The water supply may come from a stream or from surface runoff, and a dam holds the water required to suit your needs.

Concerns about the embankment pond include any negative results of interrupting the normal water flow and also taking care of any overflow in order not to stress your dam. You have to consider the drainage area below the dam as well.

If you're impounding a substantial amount of water, be sure that dam failure or excess overflow wouldn't cause any personal or property injury.

Excavated ponds are most commonly used in areas that are level. Depending on the terrain, they may be less complicated and less expensive to build.

However, in many cases, it means a "bucket of dirt for a bucket of water" in effort. And the dirt has to be moved twice, so ponds likely are small.

In many cases, no provision is made for mechanical spillways and drainage systems. This can create a problem if you ever need to drain the water for weed control, fish renovation, and curing leaks.

Dug ponds may be fed by surface water or groundwater from springs or wells. Therefore, they're subject to fluctuating water levels, which may not allow the pond owner the flexibility needed for the chosen uses.

If surface runoff is the primary water source, the excavated pond has the same requirements as the embankment pond — providing for excess water that heavy rain may bring into the pond.

In some cases, the water may need to be diverted. In others, an outflow system should be provided.

WATER OPTIONS

The quantity and quality of the water source is crucial. Usually, embankment ponds are in natural valleys at the base of a watershed or at the foot of a small stream.

And excavated ponds may be totally

Average Rainfall by State

Note: Annual rainfall varies greatly from east to west in some states. See the map on page 14.

dependent on springs, shallow groundwater, or wells.

But in a good portion of the U.S., rain and runoff water from the watershed probably will be sufficient. An adequate watershed may vary (depending on the amount of rain) from a ratio of 3 acres to 30 acres of watershed, or more, for each acre of pond.

The watershed must be large enough to maintain water in the pond during drought and to compensate for any seepage and evaporation losses. But too much water could wash out your dam, erode the banks, and dilute your fertilized water.

A number of factors determine the amount of watershed your pond will need: 1) The size of your pond; 2) your area's average annual rainfall; 3) the type of subsoil; 4) the amount and kind of vegetation; and 5) the slope of the land.

Your local offices of the NRCS and the Army Corps of Engineers have the

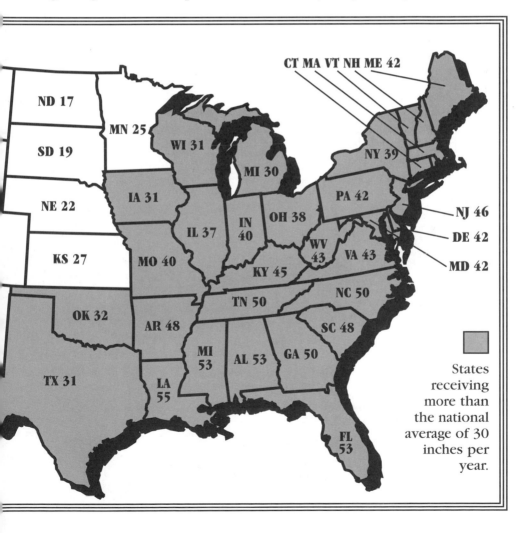

CT MA VT NH ME 42

ND 17
MN 25
WI 31
MI 30
NY 39
SD 19
IA 31
PA 42
NE 22
OH 38
IN 40
NJ 46
IL 37
DE 42
WV 43
VA 43
MD 42
KS 27
MO 40
KY 45
NC 50
OK 32
TN 50
AR 48
SC 48
MI 53
AL 53
GA 50
TX 31
LA 55
FL 53

States receiving more than the national average of 30 inches per year.

relevant data for your area. Also, a look at maps of your area will show the presence (or absence) of ponds, which may tell you a lot about your probable success in establishing a pond.

After you've located where your water is coming from, what else do you need to consider about the supply?

The use of stream water has a cou-ple of drawbacks. Diverting or stopping streams could have an effect on other property owners. Water laws ("riparian" laws) vary across the country. An investigation into local regulations that pertain to these waters will save future headaches. You may find it easier to tap into another water source.

Or you might be able to pump water from the stream into your pond. The problem with stream water, called "wild water," is that it's likely to be

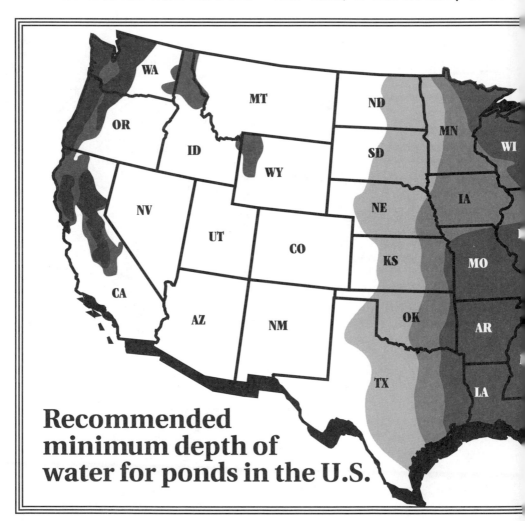

Recommended minimum depth of water for ponds in the U.S.

filled with trash fish you don't want in your fishpond. The use of filters and chemicals would be necessary to remove the wild fish and fish eggs during initial filling of the pond and during periodic replenishing.

Also, the quality of the water from a stream or from the watershed is crucial. It is muddy, it could increase the silt layer on the bottom of your pond in a short time, reducing the depth. And it would be harmful to fish production.

As we said earlier, check out the origin and pathways of your water, as far as farms, manufacturing, and other land use to see if the watershed is adding excess dirt to your water.

If your on-site observations detect a possible problem, find a solution before the actual construction begins. Consider increasing the vegetation cover or allow for a basin above the pond so the silt will settle out before reaching the pond.

The quality of well or spring water is praised by some people for healthful consumption. However, the underground water you may be counting on for your excavated pond might contain dissolved carbon dioxide, nitrogen, and iron. These elements are all lethal to fish.

Groundwater also might offer little oxygen, which is essential for fish production. Whatever your water source, it's easier to control quality before the water hits the pond than to correct problems later.

SOIL TYPE

You can't hold water in a sieve, and you sure can't keep it in a pond that's dug in porous soil. Preliminary test holes in the pond basin are crucial to determine whether that pleasant spot, rimmed with a few picturesque trees, would really make a good pond site.

Your best chance for a leak-free pond lies in appropriate soil composition. Clays and silty clays are best. Sand and sand-gravel mixes or limestone underlay are worst. There are methods you can use to treat unsuitable soil areas, but they are likely to be troublesome or expensive.

If your test shows that fine-textured clays and silty clays extend well below

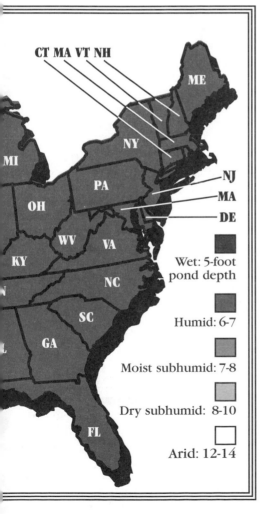

CT MA VT NH
ME
NY
MI
NJ
PA MA
OH DE
WV VA
KY
NC
SC
GA
FL

Wet: 5-foot pond depth

Humid: 6-7

Moist subhumid: 7-8

Dry subhumid: 8-10

Arid: 12-14

the proposed pond depth, you're in business. Even if it shows sandy clays for an adequate depth, you're probably safe to dig.

But if you throw all caution to the wind and insist on putting your pond where soils are predominately coarse-textured sands or sand-gravel mixtures, you're asking for trouble.

In areas with shallow soils, the rock layer below should be investigated. It may be solid and impervious or fractured and leaky. If you build on fragmented or porous rock, you could see your pond seep away into cracks that gradually develop.

However, if your soil is less than perfect and your site choices are limited, there are several sealing methods you can use that go beyond the basic compaction that is necessary for any pond.

Here is a summary of some of these techniques so you'll know what you may be letting yourself in for in order to prevent a leaky pond somewhere down the road.

The first step, compaction, is the way you prepare the basin initially in any case.

■ **Compaction:** Roll moist soil that is at least 10% clay with a wide range of particle sizes to a dense, tight layer. The compacted seal needs to be about 2 feet thick for ponds up to 10 feet deep.

■ **Clay blankets:** Use a well-graded material containing at least 20% clay to blanket the entire basin, as well as the upstream slope of the embankment. Then compact as above.

■ **Add bentonite:** This fine-textured clay absorbs several times its own weight in water. It's almost impervi-

ous to water when mixed with coarse-grained material and compacted.

Bentonite is an expensive solution. And it isn't suitable for ponds where the water level fluctuates widely. If it dries, the material shrinks to its original volume, leaving cracks.

Another drawback is its powdery texture; it can easily be blown away during application. Pond consultants often get questions about pouring bentonite through the water to seal leaky ponds, but this won't work, they say, because of its fine texture.

■ **Waterproof linings:** Probably the most expensive method, this is a relatively long-lasting solution. The cost of liners will vary by region and quality.

The success of these liners depends on proper installation. The basin floor should be cleared of all stumps, sharp rocks, and vegetation and holes filled.

If the soil is very coarse or stony, cover it with a cushion layer of sand. Lay the linings in sections or strips, allowing a 6-inch overlap for seaming.

Dig an anchor trench about 8 inches deep and about 12 inches wide all the way around the bank of the pond at or above the normal water level. Fill the trench with soil and cover the lining with about 6 inches of earth or earth mixed with gravel.

If your pond is fed by groundwater, you may be sealing out your water supply so you'll have to find another.

DETERMINING DIMENSIONS

Your intended use and the land area you have available are the basic considerations for pond size.

Maintenance requirements also are important. You might think the bigger the better until it comes time to trim weeds or fertilize fish.

USEFUL MEASUREMENTS

Acre	43,560 square feet of surface area 1 square, 208.71 feet per side A circle with diameter of 235.4 feet
Acre-foot	1 surface acre, 1 foot deep 43,560 cubic feet 325,850 gallons 2,718,144 pounds of water
Cubic foot	7.48 gallons 62.4 pounds of water
Gallon	8.34 pounds of water
1 part/million	1 ounce per 1,000 cubic feet of water

This is a good time to explain the acre-foot and other measurements you'll be using to gauge your pond's size for some purposes and management strategies.

As the table above shows, an acre-foot is 1 surface acre, 1 foot deep. The number of surface acres is the length of the pond multiplied by the width and divided by 43,560 square feet.

To calculate the surface area of an irregularly shaped pond, try looking at your pond as a triangle or circle to get an estimate.

1) Establish a base figure for a triangular computation. Multiply one-half the base footage by the height of the triangle. Divide that by 43,560 square feet and you have surface acres.

2) When the pond area more closely resembles a circle, multiply the square of the radius by 3.1416 and divide that figure by 43,560.

Whew! Now that the math lesson is out of the way, let's talk about how the use you plan for the pond will affect the size.

If your main interest is casting a line, the species of fish you plan to stock it with will have a bearing on the dimensions. Between 1 and 3 acres is a good management size for family fishing.

You need at least an acre for optimal fish balance and production, and a pond over 3 acres is liable to require more upkeep than you'd like to invest.

Bass, bluegill, and trout need an acre or more. Ponds smaller than that can't support many pounds of fish without supplemental feeding or frequent restocking. If you're limited to less than an acre, catfish might be your best low maintenance choice.

Fishponds larger than 3 acres are more expensive to manage. Although well-designed ponds as large as 20

acres are not out of the question, a series of smaller ponds may be more manageable if that much fishing area is desired.

The appropriate depth also is a consideration for fishponds, but not for the reason some fisherman think.

Some might say the fishing is better in deeper waters. In cold climates, where lakes freeze deep and summertime temperatures are relatively low, ponds do need to be deep enough to protect the fish so you'll have something to catch.

Elsewhere, a 2-acre pond, 18 feet deep, is no more productive than a 2-acre pond, 7 feet deep. The key is in the fertility, which we'll cover later in the fish management section.

The main point about depth is that you have to have enough water so fluctuations in rainfall won't create conditions that would be detrimental to fish health.

A minimum depth of 3 feet is generally recommended. This effectively discourages marginal weed growth and provides a cleaner, neater transition from land to water.

The USDA has suggestions for minimum depths of the deepest areas for the best fish cultivation. These are keyed to varying weather conditions across the country: 6 to 7 feet for most of the eastern and midwestern parts of the U.S., 7 to 8 feet from central Minnesota south through eastern Texas, 8 to 10 feet from western Minnesota through central Texas, and 12 to 14 feet for most of the rest of the country, except the Northwest and the wettest northern and central portions of California, where ponds may need to be only 5 feet deep.

If you plan to use the pond for garden irrigation or cattle watering, the size will depend on how much water you need to take care of those activities.

Consider this comparison if you're using the pond for supplemental irrigation: A healthy rainfall usually ranges from 1 to 2 inches of water per week through the principal growing season. That translates into about 28,000 gallons of water per acre, or 600 gallons for every 1,000 square feet.

You need 1 to 1.5 acre-feet of stored water for every acre you plan to irrigate. This will provide water for short-term dry spells.

A 1 acre-foot pond (with a reservoir tank specifically for irrigating) probably can take care of a garden without depleting the pond or bothering fish.

For commercial agriculture, irrigation from a pond that also serves another purpose would be limited to high-value crops on small acreages.

The amount needed for livestock depends on the number of animals and the period of time they'll be watered. Beef cattle and horses would need 12 to 15 gallons per day each, hogs about 4, and sheep about 2.

Take into consideration some seepage and evaporation loss, and you'll have a good estimate of how much storage capacity you need to allow for.

Depth also is a consideration for controlling vegetation. If you want a pond for plants, shallow depths are the rule. But unless you're planning a pond solely for waterfowl and/or plants, the water needs to be deep enough to discourage excess greenery.

So far, we've covered planning for purpose, siting, water source, and soil requirements. Now for the construction process.

BREAKING GROUND

Prior to construction, you need a written or drawn plan, showing the placements of the dam, spillway, and any other construction elements. Ask your contractor or consultant to flag those measurements on the land area so you can see how it all fits together.

Before we go into construction basics, here are a few things to think about as you're moving dirt around.

■ The shape of your pond is an initial consideration, if your site allows you some leeway. Take a tip from the surrounding landscape and echo the curves that may already exist.

■ If you dig up any good-sized rocks, save them. They can be put to use for diving platforms or fishing stations. And a cluster of rocks lying deep on the pond bed creates a cool water shelter for fish.

■ Plan now for any islands or peninsulas you'd like for visual interest or fishing convenience. But keep in mind that irregular shapes may create isolated pockets of semi-stagnant water that encourage algae and weeds.

■ Also pick out the best spot for a dock or boathouse. It's much simpler to build these structures before water fills the pond. And plan for electrical wiring and water pipes.

CLEARING

You're ready to dig or dam, and it's time to clear the site. Plan for shade for future activities before the pond is built. If possible, confine land clearing to the pond area and save any trees that won't create problems with roots in the dam or spillway. You'll appreci-

Build tree wells to protect the roots of trees you want to save.

ate the shade when summertime hits.

Excess dirt dumped over tree roots can smother them and kill the tree. Tag your favorite trees near the pond site and build tree wells if necessary to protect them during construction.

For embankment ponds, clear the dam and spillway area of trees, brush, stumps, rocks more than 6 inches in diameter, sod, and rubbish.

Always stockpile your topsoil (strip the top 12 to 18 inches). The stockpile should be outside the pond building area but near the dam site.

After the dam is built, put a 4- to 6-inch layer of topsoil on the dam top, the spillway, and the back slope. This will make it much easier for ground cover to become established.

Don't leave any vegetative material in the dam. It will decay and cause leaks and possibly lead to the collapse of your dam.

For dug ponds, some experts recommend that all excavated soil be hauled away. This can be expensive and unnecessary. Instead, spread the dirt on land adjacent to the pond site in thin layers, smoothed and grassed. Excess soil from large ponds can be used to make an island or dirt pier for fishing.

Soil that is free of vegetative matter can be used to build embankments around the excavation to help increase the water level of the pond. Tree stumps, tops, and other woody debris can be burned on-site. This may require a burn permit from local officials, but it's the cheapest way to dispose of the debris.

Make the inside slope of the pond steep enough to discourage the growth of weeds and algae. A rule of thumb is about 2 feet horizontally for each vertical foot (2:1) in dug ponds and closer to 3:1 in embankment ponds.

If you'd like a walk-in access for swimming, prepare a slope that is closer to 4:1. While you're at it, lay down a stretch of sand and create a beach. Carve out an area a couple of feet deeper than the shoreline and fill it in with sand.

This creates a pad that is easy on the feet and also mulches out aquatic weeds and algae, otherwise a potential problem in such a shallow area.

You'll have to replenish the sand every couple of years, so leave room for truck access to your beach.

Before the pond fills is the time to lime your pond basin if the initial soil test showed an acid condition. Check with your pond consultant to determine the appropriate quantity of ag limestone for your pond.

CONSTRUCTING THE DAM

One important factor in selecting an embankment pond site is the availability of good fill material for the dam. Moving material from a distance can get very expensive.

Small gravel, coarse and fine sand, and clay make the best combination, with 20% clay by weight.

USDA suggests this test for determining the content of the proposed fill:

■ Take a representative sample of the fill material and remove any gravel by passing the material through a ¼-inch sieve or screen.

■ Fill a large, straight-sided bottle to about one-third with the material and finish filling it with water. Shake the bottle vigorously for several minutes. Then, allow the soil material to settle for about 24 hours.

■ The coarse material (sand) drops to the bottom first, and finer material (clay) settles last.

■ Estimate the proportion of sand, silt, and clay by measuring the thickness of the different layers with a ruler.

Ideally, the foundation material would consist of a thick layer of consolidated clay or sandy clay.

If a suitable layer is at or near the surface, no special measures are needed. The topsoil is removed, and the area is scarified or disked to provide a bond with the soil used to build the dam.

If the foundation is sand or a sand-gravel mixture, an engineer should design the dam to prevent excessive seepage and possible failure. Keep in mind that the cost of correction may not be feasible for small ponds.

A minimum top width for dams is 6 feet if your fill height is 10 feet or less. Increase the top width as the dam height increases. If the top of the dam will be used for a road, increase the width to allow for safety. Usually a 14- to 16-foot-wide top works well. If the road will be used daily or for permanent access, consider placing the road on the backside of the dam, away from the water's edge. Always consult with an engineer and/or the county road department if you plan public access to your site.

Side slopes of the dam should be 3:1 to 4:1 for best maintenance. A tractor won't be able to traverse a slope any steeper than that to keep the grass cut.

If there's any question about the stability of the dam or if you expect heavy wave action from boating or weather, the dam should be protected.

For many small ponds, a good sod of grass on the face of the dam should control erosion from waves. But for larger dams, rocks, logs, or concrete about 2 feet above and below the waterline

During the construction process, save any good-quality topsoil to spread over the finished banks to help establish grass and prevent erosion.

along the inside face of the dam may be needed.

Any concrete work requires consultation with an engineer for proper design and installation.

CLAY TO THE CORE

The core trench of a dam is like the foundation of a building. A clay core is necessary to bond the above-ground portion of the dam to the sub-soil and should extend to the top of the dam.

This will guard against excessive seepage.

Construct the core from the best clay available, extending a minimum of 3 feet into desirable subsoil, with a width of about twice its estimated depth at any point.

In sandy soil conditions, the core trench often extends several feet into the ground to "cut off" sandy layers and to reach clay. Local experience is essential here.

Good backfill material should be placed in the core trench and around pipes and anti-seep collars.

The core trench is excavated and back-filled with compacted soil to seal off underground water flow. When the core trench is filled back to normal ground (original surface), the drainpipe is installed and the embankment is begun.

Backfill in the core trench and in the embankment should be layered in 4- to 6-inch depths and compacted. Rubber-tired equipment does a good compaction job as the fill is hauled in, but some dams may require specialized power compaction equipment or sheepsfoot rollers.

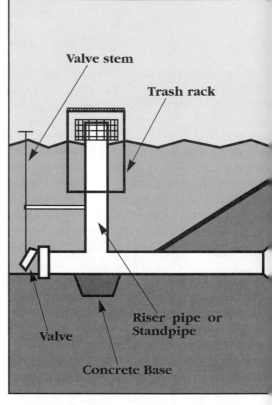

Valve stem

Trash rack

Riser pipe or Standpipe

Valve

Concrete Base

Again, use local experience as a guide.

Proper soil compaction is one of the most critical elements in dam building. This will help prevent leaks.

SPILLWAYS, DRAIN

The life of your pond could depend on a well-designed and installed spillway. Excess water needs to be directed into a runoff channel so the water in the pond doesn't rise high enough to damage the dam.

Earthen Spillway

Establish an earthen (or emergency) spillway in the embankment on the downslope side of the pond. Normally, the top of the dam will be 3 to 4 feet above water level, and the top of the

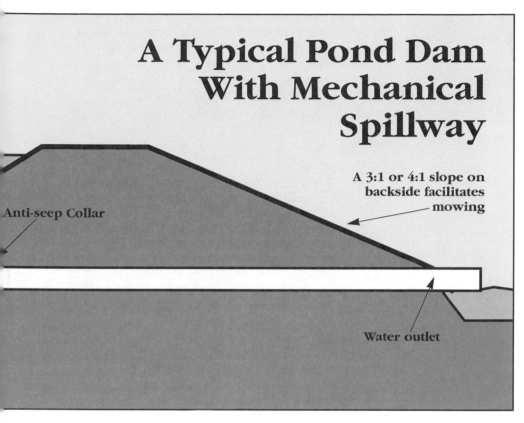

A Typical Pond Dam With Mechanical Spillway

A 3:1 or 4:1 slope on backside facilitates mowing

Anti-seep Collar

Water outlet

emergency spillway 2 feet above water.

In a well-designed pond, the emergency spillway should only carry water once or twice a year. The expected water flow will determine the width and length. In most cases, the spillway should be designed so it is able to take care of at least 2 inches of water. The more water, however, the more stabilization will be needed.

If you expect excessive amounts of overflow, you'll need to get help from a private engineer. He may recommend a concrete spillway. Such a structure should last a lifetime, but it will be much more costly than dirt and grass.

With a properly constructed spillway, you shouldn't have to worry about losing a lot of fish in the overflow. The proper width and length would keep the depth 3 inches or less for most storms.

However, some pond owners do put up spillway barriers made of welded wire, hardware cloth, or chicken wire. In a dug pond, this isn't a problem because there's no dam to be threatened with rising water levels. But for embankment ponds, these are not recommended. They can endanger the dam by trapping debris, restricting water flow, and causing water levels to rise.

Here is one relatively easy-to-build, low-maintenance parallel-bar spillway barrier that has been used successfully by embankment pond owners. It allows small debris to slip through the hori-

zontal bars but prevents the escape of harvestable fish from the pond.

The height of the barrier should be based on the individual spillway and the height of the dam.

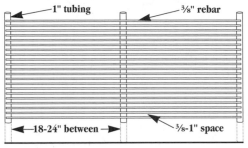

This simple-to-make barrier for an emergency spillway helps keep fish in when excess water flows through.

Primary Mechanical Spillway/Drain

A primary drain/spillway in the embankment is important for efficient pond management. If one isn't provided for in planning, the water can only be managed by pumping it in and out, which can be a major chore.

Installing a drainpipe may take additional thought during construction, but it can save you a lot of headaches in the future. It will be invaluable if you ever need to drain the pond or divert large volumes of runoff water. One expert says that for every $1 a landowner spends up front, he saves himself $10 down the road.

The underwater drain is essential for fish management. Because fish food is produced in the upper 6 feet of pond water, taking the unproductive water from the bottom is preferable to draining the nutrient-rich water from the surface. The drain is installed through the lowest point of the base of the dam.

Smooth steel, corrugated aluminum, or PVC pipe (schedule 40 or 80) are commonly used. And there may be other choices in your area. Your local contractor or NRCS office can tell you what's available.

One argument against the use of the underground drain is that pond leaks may start around the pipe. If it's installed correctly, this should not be the case.

At any rate, attention during construction can reduce the possibility of future leaks. Metal cut-offs or concrete collars should be located at intervals along the pipe, surrounded by tightly packed clay.

The advantages of the spillway/drain system far outweigh the disadvantages:
■ Provides for efficient fish production.
■ Permits water level to be lowered for weed control.
■ Speeds draining if dam needs repair.
■ Lets you reduce water to sow waterfowl food plants.
■ Allows for stock-watering tank or irrigation reservoir below the dam.

SOMETHING EXTRA

The above note leads us to a couple of added devices that can expand the usefulness of your pond water.

A simple extension of the drainpipe with an outside valve below the dam can supply a livestock watering trough. This valve also can fill an irrigation reservoir. Remember to include these uses when determining your pond capacity.

And a dry hydrant for fire protection is another bonus if your pond is located close to your house, barn, or other buildings.

The design that's right for your

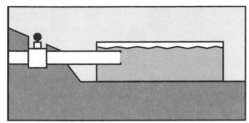

During construction, it would be simple to include plans for a reservoir and an outside value to handle livestock watering or garden irrigation.

pond will vary according to the site. An engineer should approve the specifications.

To tap into the water supply, you need to provide a centrifugal pump, with a power unit and a hose long enough to reach all sides of all the buildings, and one or more dry hydrants.

The success of the dry hydrant may depend on your water capacity. Although water storage requirements for fire protection are not large, the withdrawal rate for firefighting is high.

But in such an emergency, you're probably not worrying about the ideal conditions for your fish.

A typical firehose line running for five hours uses ¼ acre-foot of water. Check with a local dealer in pumps and engines about pump size, capacity, and engine horsepower.

And make sure the hydrant is compatible with local fire equipment and that your site provides truck access around the hydrant location in case of emergency.

THE BEST TIME TO BUILD

The best time to build is when soil and weather conditions are right. You will get a better job when the site is reasonably dry, and equipment doesn't bog down and make a mess.

If soil is excessively wet, you won't get good compaction. Ponds are permanent features in your landscape. If you have to wait six months for good working conditions, then wait.

Materials Needed for Installing a Typical Dry Hydrant

1. Six-inch schedule 40 PVC pipe usually is purchased in 21-foot lengths. The total length of the pipe depends on the distance from the water intake to the above-ground loading site. The shorter this distance, the less friction loss.
2. Two 45- or 90-degree elbow joints.
3. One threaded cleanout plug used to clean mud and trash from the water intake strainer if it gets clogged.
4. One threaded brass connection and one cap at aboveground outlet. The hookup capability of the local fire department will determine the diameter and the types of thread.
5. Sleeves to connect the 21-foot sections of

PVC pipe. The number of sleeves required will depend on the distance from the intake source to the loading site.

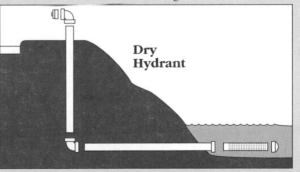

Dry Hydrant

6. A 2-foot-long strainer at the water intake. The strainer may be made of PVC pipe that has holes to prevent clogging.
7. PVC glue to cement the fittings.

Also, time your pond construction to take advantage of fish stocking dates for your area. And allow time for the pond to fill before the recommended stocking date.

Cattails can over-crowd a pond if they're not kept in check.

Public hatcheries distribute bream from November through March, so the pond would need to be completed between August and December. Early stocking allows bream to develop to reproduction size, providing food for bass that are stocked the following spring.

Several problems can develop during the initial stocking if your pond completion doesn't fit this schedule. If you finish the pond during the spring and summer, it's likely to fill with water and become contaminated and overpopulated with wild fish before the hatchery fish are available.

Also, aquatic weeds could gain a foothold during the spring and summer. And those completed during January or February may not fill in time to receive bream during the stocking season.

LANDSCAPING

When you talk about landscaping a pond or lake, it's a lot different from just prettying up the area around your house. Some details, like protecting the watershed, are musts.

Others, such as allowing for trees, walkways, or flowers, will make it a much more enjoyable place to spend time.

Give some thought to what kind of amenities and plants best fit your uses. We've already mentioned trying to save valuable trees for shade for your activities. But some experts say that decaying foliage from trees can have a detrimental effect on fish.

Also, the nutrients that a plant needs and its potential to spread may threaten your water quality. The answer might be in compromise, realizing that if you want certain plantings, you'll have some maintenance chores.

Draw a landscape design before you set out any plants. And look at the area from several different angles. Consider the potential tree size in a few years when you plant a tiny sapling. Use large trees to "frame" the pond, not obscure it.

Growing Tips

Up front, you felt very lucky that your soil had just the right amount of clay to make a good pond. But normally that is same type of soil that will rim your pond, and did you every try to grow prize-winning petunias in clay? It's not a good medium for plants.

If you saved some good topsoil when you cleared your land, lay it around the perimeter. You'll stand a better chance of getting vegetation started quickly to prevent erosion of the banks and dam.

But chances are, you didn't have good-quality topsoil either. Get a soil test to see what nutrients you need.

Although you don't want to add any elements that might wash into the pond and affect the quality of the water, it's most important to establish ground cover as soon as possible.

Grass

The first priority, and a very important one, is to establish a good stand of grass to protect the shoreline and dam from eroding.

Your district conservationist can recommend a grass, a grass/legume mixture, or a legume that best suits your area. When ponds are finished during cold weather, a temporary mulch of straw, bark, or jute netting or a short-term planting of fast-growing ryegrass or other similar plant will help protect the soil.

Other good choices for permanent pond-bank plantings include tall fescue, weeping lovegrass, sericea lespedeza, crownvetch, white clover, and various mixtures of these seed for sunny, dry sites; creeping red fescue for shady, dry sites; tall fescue/creeping red fescue and creeping red fescue/Lathco flat pea mixtures for partial shade; and Reed canarygrass for wet banks.

Shrubs, trees

Adding trees and shrubs around the pond can help it blend into the setting and make the area more appealing for recreation.

If you want your pond to appear larger, the fewer trees and the more sky reflected in the water will do the trick. Fill in tree bases with a few ferns.

A shapely weeping willow swaying in the breeze paints its own picture. But they're invasive; do not use them near drain tile lines.

Or you might prefer stately magnolias. These trees, as well as water oaks,

---

Here are a few considerations for greening up your pond perimeter:

1. Lay sod in erodible areas. You may have to scarify or loosen the earth if it's compacted to give sod roots a place to go. You need a 4- to 6-inch layer prepared for planting.

2. Select plants that are natural to your location. Look around; what trees and shrubs do you see?

3. Check the pH of the area to be planted. Pond building exposes subsoil layers that often are acidic. Apply limestone to adjust the pH to 6.0.

4. Set plants that must have fertilizer in a slight depression so the nutrients have less chance of running into the pond.

5. Choose plants that can tolerate wet soil because the soil around the pond is likely to be very moist below the surface.

6. Confine optional plants to the best soil areas.

Laurel oaks, yellow poplar, red maple, and bald cypresses make good water companions.

Among shrubs, wax myrtle, waxleaf ligustrum, and Burford, dwarf Chinese, yaupon, and dwarf yaupon hollies are good choices. Yellowroot (a low, deciduous shrub) is ideal for wet, shady places and has an attractive fall leaf color.

If you'd like azaleas, hybrid rhodendendron, or dogwood, plant them well back from the pond's edge, and, if possible, on higher ground. These plants must have well-drained soil to survive.

Other plants that don't like wet feet include boxwood, common camellia, sasanqua camellia, Japanese cleyera, junipers, ornamental cherry, and roses.

Never plant trees and shrubs on the dam or spillway. Their roots will weaken the structure and cause deterioration or collapse.

Finally, remember that while too much shrubbery at the pond's edge might get in the way of fishing, a shade tree or two can make hours spent with pole in hand a lot more comfortable.

Flowers, Ornamental Grasses

Don't want to stop with the basics? Consider some attractive extras. Plant wildflowers to attract butterflies and birds. Many native weeds that commonly grow around pond edges are food for caterpillar larvae.

Arrowhead, iris, and daylilies are very compatible with wet sites. But bog plants can take over a pond. Check with your local nursery or pond experts to see which ones could become problems for you.

Pampas grass, daylilies, and ferns are also good pond companions. They thrive in wet ground.

Other ornamental grasses for full sun, wet conditions are variegated grassy-leaved sweet flag (*Acorus*), Japanese silver grass (*Miscanthus*), switchgrass (*panicum*), and prairie cordgrass (*Spartina*).

Aquatic Plants

Get aquatic plants from a reputable source. Digging your own from another pond runs the risk of bringing noxious plants such as pondweeds into your pond.

And although the water lily has been revered in some circles for almost 4,000 years and members of Egyptian royal families were buried

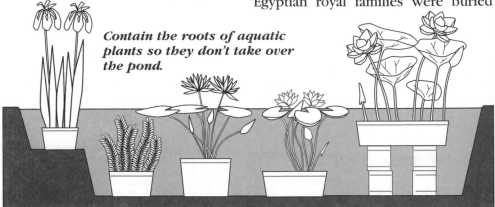

Contain the roots of aquatic plants so they don't take over the pond.

with their petals, they're just nuisances to many pond owners.

Unless you're specializing in a water garden with lilies and lotuses, as well as the lowly cattail, take precautions to limit their growth. Plant them in 5-gallon containers filled with soil. As they only grow in water less than 3 feet deep, provide a stump or blocks to set them on.

Remove the containers before applying any chemicals that your pond may need to control unwanted aquatic growth.

Plants for Wildlife

Want to double your fun with a wildlife area? That will work, if you've declared swimming off-limits anyway.

You can develop a pond to include habitats for wildlife, as well as fish. One problem may be if you attract waterfowl that like the taste of your fish. While not an everyday threat, a cormorant can eat a pound of fish at each feeding. And small fish make good meals for herons, egrets, and kingfishers.

An ideal wildlife situation would be a pond area that can be drained during the summer to plant or encourage vegetation that will attract fall migrating birds after it is flooded again.

Shallow areas with water between 6 inches and 3 feet are necessary for the aquatic plants that wild birds want — sage pondweed, wild celery, coontail, elodea, arrowhead, wild Japanese millet, lotus, water lily, iris, pickerel rush, and burr reed.

And you need to include at least one area of gravel that birds can get to for the required grit for digestion.

Welcome wildfowl to your pond by preparing suitable food areas.

For deer, plant perennial legumes such as red and white clover, bird's-foot trefoil, and alfalfa in upland areas. White clover is the best choice for a wetter site.

Boat Docks and Storage

The best time to pick a place for piers or boat docks and boat storage is while your pond is still in the planning phase.

You may want just a simple fishing pier. With a little more effort, you can expand the floor and add a roof to double your fun.

Or you believe that the size of your pond or lake and the scope of your activities will require a more elaborate storage, docking, and fishing facility like this one designed by William L. Mattison, an architect in Monroe, La. It includes a covered boat slot, indoor storage, and built-in benches.

Whatever structures you decide on, it's easier to get them started before the pond fills up. A couple of reminders: 1) Plan for electrical and water needs early on. 2) Be sure to use lumber that has been treated to be freshwater resistant.

Completing the Landscape

A bridge could be a useful or attractive addition to your pond landscape. Stone, steel, or iron ones will last longer, but they also will be more expensive. A simple wooden structure will do if it's sturdy and mounted on stone or concrete. And make the bridge longer than it's needed to allow for possible bank erosion.

For safety's sake, add a handrail, particularly if children and older folks will be using it. Scour walking surfaces occasionally with a stiff wire brush to keep them clean and slip-free.

Also provide for paths so you can survey your domain at close hand.

Use those large rocks you might have uncovered while excavating to build diving or fishing platforms or

Double your fun with a boathouse that features storage areas and space for relaxation.

steps down into the water.

You might create a rock-based waterfall that could serve two purposes. It looks outstanding as the water cascades over it into the pond, and it may also provide additional oxygen for the fish.

PURELY PLEASURE

As you make the decisions about sit-ing, building, and landscaping your pond, keep in mind your reasons for wanting a water attraction in the first place—pleasure. Plan it so that maintenance chores can be kept to a minimum.

If you have to spend all your time cleaning, clearing, and keeping up, you won't have a chance to stretch out on the bank and count the katydids.

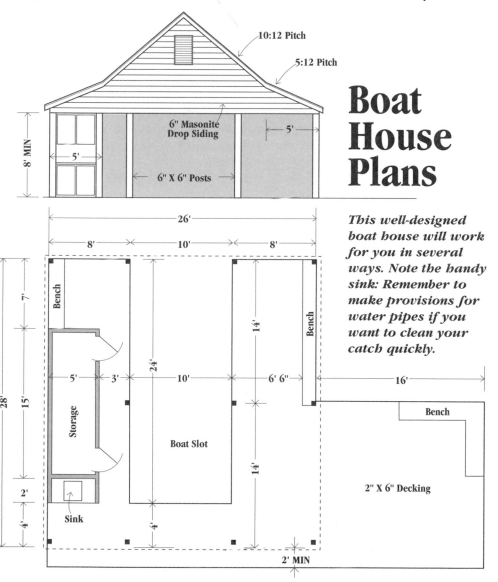

Boat House Plans

This well-designed boat house will work for you in several ways. Note the handy sink: Remember to make provisions for water pipes if you want to clean your catch quickly.

Maintaining Your Interest

Points to Pond-er

▶ Watch for any signs of erosion of watershed or damage to the dam.

▶ Repair leaks as soon as possible.

▶ Regulate plants on the pond bank and in the water.

▶ Stock the fish your pond can support.

▶ Maintain a healthy habitat.

▶ Record your catch.

II.

MAINTAINING

The pond owner's job often is just beginning when construction is complete. The contractor has gone home and your friends from the NRCS and state fisheries office are working on someone else's pond.

Now it's up to you to be the watchdog to ensure the success of your well-built waterhole.

And going back to our basic building strategies: Good construction practices will make your maintenance job much easier.

A variation on an old saying makes the best point about solving pond problems: "If you don't have time [and money] to do it right the first time, how will you have time [and money] to do it over?"

The basic maintenance plan you initiate for your pond needs to include several essential elements.

And there are additional tasks that will be required, depending on how you plan to use the pond.

POND UPKEEP

First, you have to take care of the pond itself. Doing what's necessary to keep the dam, banks, and watershed in

Cattle can damage the bank and muddy the water, resulting in poor conditions for a recreational pond. Fence them out and provide a watering tank.

good shape is vital for overall success.

Here are some key points that will help you develop your strategies.

Make a checklist for regular maintenance and include the following.

■ Remove volunteer trees from the dam. Keep the dam and spillway area in grass sod and mowed.

■ Examine dams and spillways for signs of erosion. Fill any openings with good-quality clay, compact it, and reseed ground cover.

■ Clean trash racks, valves, and watering troughs frequently.

■ Watch out for damage from livestock or wildlife.

Some other common pond maintenance problems need in-depth attention.

STOPPING LEAKS

The surest way to keep your pond from leaking is (no surprise here) to adhere to basic construction essentials that you may be inclined to skimp on to save time and/or money: testing soil, clearing vegetation, and installing the drainpipe correctly.

Lower water levels don't always mean that you have a leak. A new pond may seep a little until the soil settles.

Also, take into consideration any additional use, livestock or irrigation, that may be depleting your supply.

Or perhaps your water supply isn't adequate for normal fluctuations. Even in humid areas, you could lose as much as 18 inches of water a year from evaporation. If this loss isn't offset by normal rainfall, your pond level will drop.

Dug ponds, which rely on ground-water, will fluctuate up and down by season as the groundwater (usually highest in the spring and lowest in the fall) rises and falls. This is normal, and you can offset the problem with supplemental well water.

You can't tell what normal seasonal variations may be until you've watched the pond for at least a year. And check out your neighbors' ponds to see if they're also below normal levels.

However, if water levels drop during periods of good weather conditions and average use, you may have a leak. And most often, leaks develop because of porous soil, tree root deterioration, or improper drainpipe installation.

The drainpipe is the first place many people inspect for leaks. Aquatic vegetation, such as cattails, growing below the dam suggests leakage.

The surest way to correct any leak is to drain the pond, locate the rupture, and plug it. A pond consultant or your local NRCS can give you more information about what has worked on ponds in your area. Some leaks are difficult to find and advice from an expert will help.

If you determine that the leak is because of porous soil, several techniques for correcting it were discussed in the "Building" section.

The need to contain toxic wastes has spurred research into new methods of sealing landfills and lagoons. Some of these strategies are adaptable to farm ponds.

An oil field equipment company that sells barite, bentonite, and plastic liners may be able to help you find the materials you need. However these artificial aids will only work if they're installed properly, and they are expensive.

When it's not practical to drain the pond, barite can be poured into the water over the suspected leak. Barite is a clay substance similar to bentonite but about twice as heavy.

The barite forms a gel-like barrier and plugs leaking soils. For small leaks in dikes, 1 to 3 pounds of barite per surface acre should work. It will not seal holes caused by muskrats or beavers. Portland cement can be mixed into the soil or poured through the water like barite. The application rate is the same.

You are the only one who can decide how much time and money you want to invest in correcting a leak. And sometimes ponds even repair themselves.

If nothing seems to work and you still really want that water attraction, you might consider digging a well to keep it supplied.

DECREASING SILT

Silting in of ponds is a fact of life. As sediment collects from decaying vegetation and soil that is picked up by runoff from heavy rains, the depth decreases.

However, you have some control over how long your pond lasts by finding out the source of the sediment that's settling into the pond basin.

Watershed is the main culprit. If your upland area is eroding, you'll end up with muddy water. (Muddy water also is detrimental to your fish population.) A well-forested watershed is the best protection from upland erosion.

If you're in a developing watershed,

new homes, roads, and other construction can increase silt problems. This usually is temporary, and most areas in the country now require a builder to control sediment on-site.

If you live in a farming community or where dirt roads are common, you'll have sediment problems annually. The best defense is a wooded or grass buffer all around the pond edge, usually 50 feet wide. This buffer will filter out most sediment before it reaches your pond.

Most of the time, you won't control all the activities in your watershed. If

If cropland uphill from your pond is eroding, you're likely to end up with muddy water.

the problem is severe in a certain area and you have adequate watershed otherwise, you may have to permanently terrace upland and divert the runoff.

Or consider putting a sedimentation basin above the pond that will trap the silt-laden water. A grass-covered spill-

way or pipe can be used to connect the water areas.

You do have control over the area around the new pond that may be contributing unwanted sediment. To aid in combatting erosion along the banks, a good quality topsoil that will allow ground cover to become established is a must.

In small erosion-prone areas, hay bales can filter runoff while temporary terraces also help. And a variety of landscape netting is available that will hold soil.

Excess sediment also could be coming from banks and dams that have been eroded by wind and waves. Check out these areas, and if you find any damage, take immediate action to correct the problem by covering the area with rocks (or concrete, if necessary) above and below the water line.

(Here we go, back to "Building" again.)

If you use the pond for cattle, their hooves and heavy weight can cause a lot of damage to the banks, and that will increase sediment in the pond. Consider fencing them out and add the outside value and water trough described earlier.

Excessive decaying vegetation, which also adds to the sedimentation layer, can be prevented by keeping pond sides steep enough to discourage weed growth. Also, read on for more tips in "Taming Weeds."

TAMING WEEDS

It's been said that a weed is just a plant in the wrong place. Whether on the bank or in the water, anything that detracts from your pond fun is a weed.

Along the pond bank, the same positive elements that nourish your magnolias and daylilies (sun and water) can cause problems by also increasing

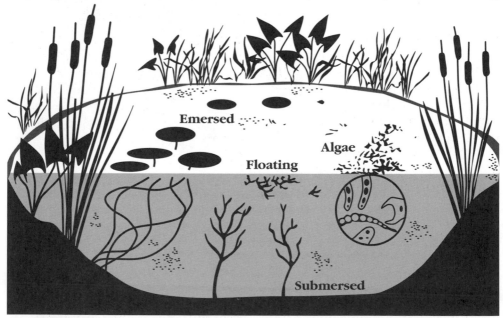

Identify your weeds by one of these four basic types to determine the best chemical treatment.

weedy growth that creates a haven for insects and poisonous reptiles.

This growth also harbors resting and nesting places for frogs and waterfowl. But you'd think twice about sidling up to a pond that is completely surrounded by 3-foot-high vegetation.

Regulate weeds on the banks by mowing, creating shady areas, and mulching, just like in the vegetable garden. Chemicals may offer a speedy solution, but consult the experts about any effect its use will have on aquatic vegetation.

Now to tackle the tough stuff, aquatic plants, or pond scum to the testy fisherman. Excess filamentous algae or duckweed can swallow your fishing line and tangle your propeller. Normally, vegetation should cover no more than 20 to 30% of the water area. Aquatic plants may include beneficial growth such as phytoplankton algae, which provides shelter and food for fish, and also waterlilies that have eye-catching blooms.

But benefits aside, anything that overpowers your water area has become a weed.

A lot of problems can be prevented by steep banks and proper fertilization. (See "Fish Management.")

Rooted aquatic weeds, as well as algae, usually begin growing in shallow water (less than 2 feet deep). Deepen the edges of new and renovated ponds to avoid shallow water. Generally, a 3-foot-deep edge will keep

the pond bottom shaded and discourage weed germination.

As time goes on, though, a combination of weed fixes usually is required, including chemical, mechanical, and biological controls.

If you haven't noticed how bad the weeds have gotten until you're ready

Water lilies that start out beautifying the pond can spread so much they become nuisances.

to spend time in the boat or on the bank looking for fun, chemical treatment may be called for.

Start by identifying the green stuff so you'll know how to handle it.

Aquatic plants are classified by four basic types: 1) algae; 2) floating weeds (duckweed, water hyacinths); 3)

emersed or above water weeds (water lilies, alligatorweed, cattails, grasses); 4) submersed or underwater weeds (bushy pondweed, watermilfoil, hydrilla).

Most Extension and state resource offices have booklets to help identify aquatic weeds for a nominal fee. If you can't identify the plant after consulting all the sources, take a sample to those offices.

Microscopic, or planktonic, algae form the beginning of the food chain, converting nutrients from the water into food for insects and fish.

It only presents a problem if it's overfertilized. Desired levels of planktonic algae are characterized by a distinct green tint to the water. Visibility less than 12 to 18 inches suggests overfertilization. The result is excessive blooming, which can deplete the oxygen that fish need.

On the other hand, filamentous algae is visible to the naked eye and often present problems. Called "pond moss," the floating mats of thread-like filaments begin growing on the pond bottom in shallow water and later float to the surface.

Helpful Herbicides

For filamentous algae, as well as the other types of water weeds, chemical treatment is the first thing that comes to mind for a quick fix.

If you choose this method, identify the weed and call your local fisheries

Weedy undergrowth encourages mosquitos and snakes, not your favorite fishing companions.

consultant for suggestions for an appropriate herbicide program. State regulations vary about chemical use.

Apply herbicides according to label instructions and note restrictions about irrigation, livestock watering,

Herbicide Suggestions for Weed Control*

Aquatic group and weed		copper sulfate	2,4-D	diquat	endothall
Algae	microscopic (plankton)	E		F	G
	filamentous	E		F	G
	chara	E		G	G
	nitella	E		G	G
Floating Weeds	duckweeds		G	E	
	coontail		G	E	E
	bladderwort			E	G
	water hyacinth		E	E	
Emersed Weeds	American lotus		E		G
	fragrant and white water lily		E		G
	spatterdock		E		G
	watershield		E		G
	water pennywort			E	
	frogbit		E	E	
	pickerelweed		G		
	alligatorweed		G		
	smartweed		E		G
	arrowhead		E	G	G
	water primrose		E	F	
	cattails		G	G	
	sedges and rushes		E	F	
	slender spikerush			G	
	buttonbush		E	F	
	willows		E	F	
	alders		E	F	
	maidencane			F	
Submersed Weeds	naiads			E	E
	parrotfeather		E	E	E
	eurasian watermilfoil		E	E	E
	broadleaf watermilfoil			E	E
	egeria			G	E
	elodea			E	F
	hydrilla	F		G	G
	fanwort				E
	pondweeds			G	E

These basic herbicides have been successful in the treatment of a number of frequently appearing weeds.

*E=excellent control; G=good control; F=fair control
Herbicides registered for aquatic uses by the Federal Government. States may have additional aquatic use restrictions.

and swimming.

And a couple of cautions: Copper, including herbicides and algicides that contain copper and copper compounds, is particularly toxic to fish. Also, the decaying vegetation from any chemical treatment could deplete the oxygen content in the water.

Oxygen depletion is more likely if chemicals are applied during hot weather. The warmer the water, the less dissolved oxygen it contains. Improper treatment can result in a fish kill. (See "Fish Management.")

However, many herbicide labels suggest application during the hottest, sunniest part of the day. The possibility of a fish kill may be decreased by treating only one-fourth to one-half of the pond at a time and waiting 14 days between treatments.

Hands-on Treatment

Raking is one way to clear floating and bottom-rooted weeds from shallow spots or beach areas of ponds.

Mechanical harvesters that cut or drag weeds are available for larger bodies of water. But they're expensive and not usually feasible for private pond owners.

You might want to try weeding by hand or using a tractor to pull chains or bedsprings through shallow areas.

The advantage is that you can work off a lot of aggravation about missing your fishing time. But the disadvantages are that it's only a temporary solution and the decomposition of plant fragments left in the water may deplete dissolved oxygen. Also, fragments can form roots and spring up in new areas if they live.

Seasonal Water Reduction

For serious weed problems, a drawdown may be necessary. If you decrease the water level of your pond for two to four consecutive years (from late fall until late winter), as much as 90% of submerged vegetation can be wiped out.

Reduce the water surface area by at least one-third and not more than one-half. But don't reduce water level in warm weather or in ponds smaller than 1 acre.

Long-Term Solution

Your best bet for eliminating unwanted submersed weeds and filamentous algae is to stock grass carp (or white amur, an Asian minnow). This long, slender silver-colored fish has large throat teeth that help it tear and shred plant material.

Grass carp do not normally reproduce in ponds or lakes, but some states prohibit them, and others require that they be certified as triploid (nonreproducing) varieties.

These are highly recommended for long-lasting (5 to 8 years) biological control, but you won't see results until the second year.

The effectiveness of grass carp depends on the stocking rate and size. They need to be large enough to avoid becoming part of the diet of your sport fish.

Other biologicals, including moths, weevils, and the alligatorweed flea beetle (which is credited with combatting alligatorweeds in Florida), are already at work in U.S. waterways.

Because of environmental concerns, check with your local pond consultant or fisheries specialist about rates and rules.

Grass carp are recommended for effective long-term weed control.

It may take more than one method of treatment and a few years' wait to find the solution that fits your needs, but you'll be paid back for your efforts many times in better fishing.

CONTROLLING TROUBLEMAKERS

Some of the pests that plague your pond might be those friends who have become much bigger buddies since you added your fishing hole. We don't have any good solutions for getting rid of them except for you to buy them a copy of this book so they can build their own pond.

But for winged and four-legged wildlife, keeping vegetation cleared and following good building practices up front are two deterrents.

Beavers, Muskrats, and Otters

Beavers dam, muskrats burrow, and otters eat your fish. Even though they're part of the pond ecology, they can become nuisances. And there are no simple solutions.

Trapping often is the only effective control. Depending on the current value of pelts, you might be able to get someone to do this for you. Trapping is more effective when everyone in the watershed participates. But it's difficult to get cooperation from all.

Muskrats are drawn to areas with an abundance of woody brush and vegetation for them to use to build nests. The dam, in particular, should be kept frcc of this type of vegetation.

Beavers are attracted by the trees at

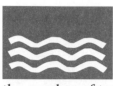
the pond site and by flowing water. They may be discouraged by eliminating or reducing the number of trees available.

Also, using a siphon system for your overflow/drainpipe makes it difficult for beavers to locate the flowing water.

Occasionally, deterrent devices for these animals hit the market and meet with varying amounts of success. Talk to neighbors who've had similar problems and see what worked for them.

Mosquitos

These annoying, potentially disease-carrying pests can ruin a twilight fishing expedition or early morning swim. You might not be able to totally eliminate them, but you can cut down on their breeding places.

The suggestions we made about construction would eliminate a couple of trouble spots: shallow water areas that encourage weed growth and drainage areas that retain water.

In addition, be on the lookout for any depressions along the bank that might hold water. It only takes a few days of standing water to produce a crop of insects.

Also, mow the pond edges regularly. Keeping grass cut will help reduce populations of mosquitos, as well as ticks and chiggers. Top-feeding fish, such as bream and Gambusia minnows, are effective in controlling mosquito larvae.

For infants or anyone who's potentially allergic to insect bites, keep the insect repellent handy. And if you live in a malarial area, it's extremely important that you follow your state health regulations for managing mosquitos.

Snakes

Keeping pond margins clean and neatly trimmed reduces hiding places for snakes.

To reduce the scare factor, spend some time with your family in learning to identify the various kinds of snakes. The vast majority are not poisonous and keep mice and rodent populations down.

Those poisonous snakes that are most likely to find their way to your pond are relatives of the rattlesnake: water moccasins (also called cottonmouths) and copperheads.

Copperheads are partial to forests. In most areas, they're brightly colored with a reddish head and brownish crossbands on the body.

Water moccasins are found in marshes or along streams where their preferred prey, frogs and fish, abound. They're called cottonmouths because of the cotton-white interior of the mouth.

Adults are usually 3 to 3½ feet. The pattern is dull and inconspicuous, consisting of dark-brown bars or blotches on a somewhat lighter background. Sometimes, they appear almost a uniform blackish.

If you don't want to take a chance on any snakes joining in your fun, there are snake "fences" available from pond suppliers that tangle the reptile so you can remove or dispose of it.

Some people make a sport of shooting reptiles, turtles, or beavers. This is dangerous and not an effective way to control pests.

When bullets hit the water surface, they skip or ricochet. And shooting around the pond shouldn't be looked on as a water sport.

Turtles

A common belief is that turtles are responsible for the disappearance of lots of fish from the pond. However, recent studies show that their diets contain less than 5% fish, and most of those fish are dead when the turtles find them.

A worse problem is a small turtle getting into the overflow pipe and blocking water flow.

If turtles are numerous enough to ter-

Water moccasins are recognizable by their lack of coloring. They're blackish, and sometimes dark-brown bars or blotches are visible.

rorize your swimmers, bite your bait, and strip your stringer, trap them so you can carry them away or turn them into soup.

A simple trap is a wire cylinder, made like a fish trap. The cylinder is about 18 inches in diameter with funnel on one end and a door on the other. The opening is oval shaped, about 5 inches high and 14 inches wide. Chicken necks or dead fish can be used for bait.

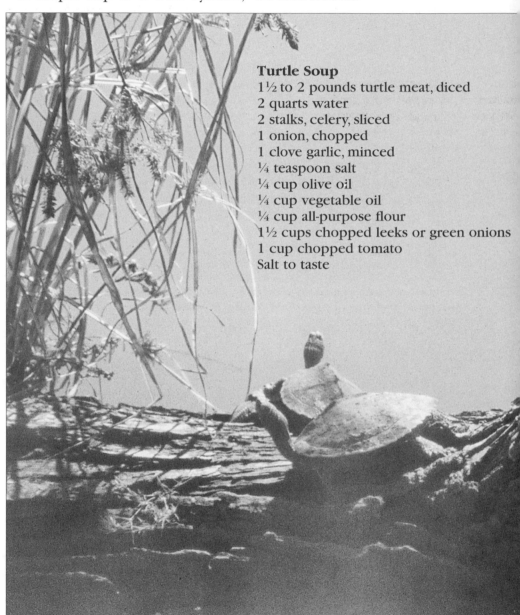

Turtle Soup
1½ to 2 pounds turtle meat, diced
2 quarts water
2 stalks, celery, sliced
1 onion, chopped
1 clove garlic, minced
¼ teaspoon salt
¼ cup olive oil
¼ cup vegetable oil
¼ cup all-purpose flour
1½ cups chopped leeks or green onions
1 cup chopped tomato
Salt to taste

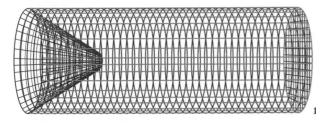

Set this kind of trap in a shallow area so the top part is out of the water; otherwise, all of the turtles that you catch will drown. A trotline, baited with chicken necks, works well to remove snapping turtles.

Combine turtle meat, water, celery, onion, garlic, and ¼ teaspoon salt in a 4-quart Dutch oven; heat to boiling. Reduce heat; simmer 30 minutes. Heat oil in medium skillet until warm. Stir in flour; cook over low heat, stirring constantly, until flour is browned. Add leeks and tomato; cook, stirring frequently, until leeks are lightly browned. Stir flour mixture into hot broth; cook until thickened and bubbly. Add salt to taste; stir in additional water if soup is too thick. Yield: about 8 servings.

FISH MANAGEMENT

Now you have the pond, and you have the basic knowledge to keep it up. Here comes the part you've been waiting for if you decided up front that your prime interest in having a pond is to have your own place for sport fishing.

But before you dump in any fingerlings, it's vital to get to know how a pond works and how plankton, water quality, and fish population determine pond productivity. There are regional variations with weather, water availability, and soil and water characteristics, but pond dynamics remain the same.

The still, unruffled waters of a pond hide an abundance of active plants and animals. The term plankton designates all microscopic and near-microscopic creatures that float in the water. Zooplankton are animals and phytoplankton is algae.

Phytoplankton algae makes up the first link in the food chain.

Zooplankton and aquatic insects feed on algae and become food for small fish. Finally, the smaller fish are eaten by larger fish and then by the fisherman.

The amount of oxygen and the pH (acidity and alkalinity) level are crucial to fish production. Keeping a certain balance is essential in maintaining the food chain.

Water with a pH less than 7.0 is considered acid, a pH greater than 7.0 indicates an alkaline condition. An early morning pH reading of 6.5 to 8.5 is most favorable for fish production.

Another way to determine the water makeup is to monitor the alkalinity.

An alkalinity level of less than 20 parts per million suggests a need to apply lime. Liming at a rate of 2 to 5 tons per surface acre is generally sufficient to raise alkalinity to the desired level.

During photosynthesis, which is prompted by sunlight, plants produce oxygen while manufacturing food from carbon dioxide and water. Then they release the oxygen into the pond water. Fish, insects, zooplankton, bacteria, and algae consume oxygen in respiration.And respiration and photosynthesis change the pH daily.

It's easy to see why good fishing doesn't just happen. Keeping all the elements in balance is the key to a successful fish pond.

> More than 90% of the failures of fish ponds are reported to be the result of the following (in order of most occurrences).
>
> **1.** Competition with fish that either are not eliminated from the pond before it is stocked with hatchery fish or that enter the pond after it is stocked with hatchery fish.
> **2.** Removing too many fish or fishing prior to the time the originally stocked bass spawn.
> **3.** Improper fertilization.
> **4.** Fish kills as a result of pesticides and natural causes.
> **5.** Inappropriate stocking.

Most of the headaches on the above list could be cured by following good management strategies. Let's start with stocking your new pond.

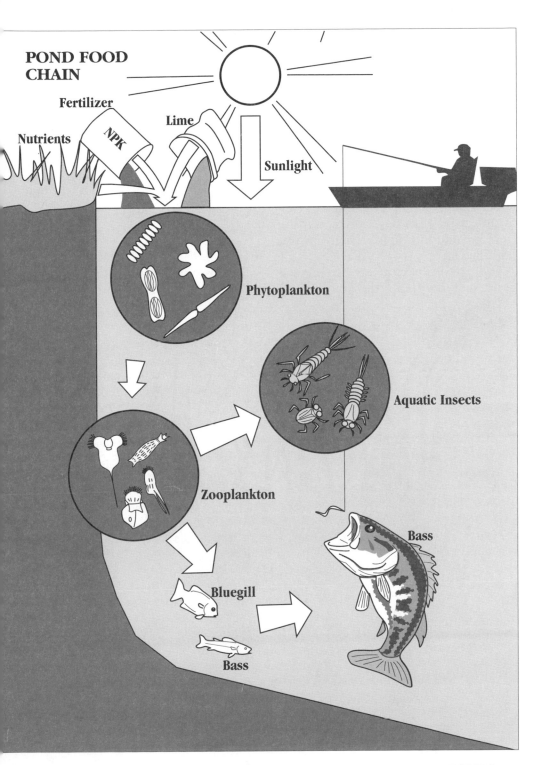

POND FOOD CHAIN

Fertilizer

Nutrients

NPK

Lime

Sunlight

Phytoplankton

Aquatic Insects

Zooplankton

Bluegill

Bass

Bass

STOCKING

If a pond is to produce a good crop of fish, it must be stocked with the right proportion of the right fish species. For this reason, all unwanted fish must be destroyed. Any unwanted fish, no matter what the species, is called a wild fish.

We're going to assume that the water that is filling your pond is free of any wild fish, and you're starting from ground zero in building your fish population.

The physical characteristics of your pond will determine the amount and type of fish you stock. The "carrying capacity" and the variety are influenced by your climate and the nutrients that are available.

In the "Building" section, we talked about suitable pond surface sizes and depths for certain fish. Most people want a recreational fish pond to give them good fishing with as little effort as possible.

The following are suggestions for the best ways to meet those objectives.

WHICH FISH TO CHOOSE

The formula for stocking is simple, but your success is dependent on tak-

ing it a step at a time.

Throwing in a few adult fish won't work. There's no way to predict the first-year production of those fish and, therefore, the continued life of the fish population.

Choosing a specific stocking strategy, based on what has worked in the past for others, gives you the best chance of ending up with the kind of fishing you want.

To manage your pond for trophy bass or channel catfish food production, you need specialized programs. A pond consultant or fisheries specialist can help you set up a plan.

For all-around good fishing, though, a largemouth bass/bluegill combination is hard to beat. It's been shown to give continued good fishing with the least amount of interference by the pond owner.

And the addition of some channel catfish for fishing variety won't affect bass and bream production, if they're stocked at recommended rates.

Bass/Bluegill

Bass is the common name for several spiny-finned fishes. In our stocking recommendations, we're talking about largemouth bass.

Bluegill, also called bream, is a freshwater sunfish.

The bass/bluegill system is simple and efficient. And it's been proven to be an effective combination across the U.S.

Here's how it works: Bass fry and all sizes of bluegill feed on zooplankton and insect larvae.

Bluegill will reproduce and grow rapidly with the abundant food and provide excellent forage for bass.

Bass will keep bluegill from over-populating, if they are not over-harvested. And some large bluegill will survive bass predation to provide good bluegill angling.

The best plan for the bluegill/bass mix is to stock ¾-inch bluegill fry in the fall. When the water warms in the spring, they're ready to spawn, and the bass stocked in early summer will have newly hatched bluegills to eat.

Sunfish and Hybrids

Another sunfish, redear, is sometimes substituted for bluegill because it seldom overpopulates. Redear also is called a shellcracker. It resembles the bluegill, but the back part of the gill cover is bright orange-red.

Fishing consultants advise against stocking other sunfish varieties such as longear, warmouth, pumpkinseed, orange-spotted, and green sunfish.

Green sunfish and warmouth are aggressive feeders and compete with bass and bluegill for food. If they get big enough, they even eat small bass.

Sunfish hybrids are sometimes used instead of bluegills where bass and bluegill are stocked at the same time. This is because the rapid reproduction rate of bluegills can result in too many fish for the available food supply, and the bluegills may become stunted.

A cross of female green sunfish and male bluegills produce offspring that are 95% male hybrids, so the reproduction rate is reduced.

Some fishermen contend that the

 hybrids make good fishing because they grow so fast and they fight respectably. But you may not want to invest the time and effort they require to maintain a supply.

Since hybrids aren't likely to replace those that fishermen take, periodic replenishing is necessary.

And because fingerlings make handy prey for bass, the additions need to be grown in cages, raceways, or separate ponds until they're 5 inches or longer. This also will require additional feeding.

Check with your local pond or fisheries consultant to see if hybrids are a viable option for you.

Catfish

Channel catfish often are added to the bass/bluegill combination for additional fishing interest. The best results are reported when 8- to 10-inch catfish are added to the pond one year after the bass are introduced.

Because catfish don't normally reproduce in farm ponds, supplementary stocking will need to be done at two- to three-year intervals. And these additions need to be at least 8 inches to reduce their chances of being food for the bass.

Newly constructed ponds usually don't provide a catfish's preferred spawning spot, a hollow log or undercut bank. To encourage reproduction, you could give them a substitute: Place sections of large diameter field tile or culvert at depths of 3 to 4 feet.

Because of those predatory bass, however, this will not guarantee more catfish for your hook.

Minnows

Stocking fathead minnows may provide a suitable food supplement for bass.

If fathead minnows are added in February, they'll spawn and provide a horde of fry for the bass and bluegills to eat, keeping them from competing with each other for available food, which is usually tiny water animals and insects.

The drawback can be if minnows are not eaten by larger fish, they might become so abundant they consume food that bream need. This is especially true in ponds with lots of aquatic growth cover where they can hide from largemouth bass and continue to reproduce.

Grass Carp

Grass carp, or white amur, are considered a good biological alternative to herbicides for weed control. However, they're not allowed in some states. (See "Taming Weeds.") If you want to use them, refer to local stocking practices.

Trout

Two factors influence the stocking of trout in farm ponds. One is water temperature, which needs to be 65° F or less. The other is that they do not reproduce in ponds and need to be restocked.

In warmer climates, trout can be stocked in the late fall when the water temperature has dropped. If they begin as 7- to 9-inch fingerlings, they can grow to 1 pound by March.

Their growth will depend on the supply of insect larvae and small bream, with a supplement of commercial fish feed. For larger trout by spring, stock larger fingerlings.

Good fishing can be had in March and April, but trout will die as water temperatures reach 70° F.

In cooler climates, they must be stocked every two or three years for harvesting. Stocking size and rates will depend on climate and predation.

Problem Fish

Crappies are OK in large lakes but not in small ponds. They prey on small bass, compete for food with adult bass and bluegill, and tend to overpopulate. This produces a pond full of small, slow-growing crappies.

Perch also do not make good companions for bass and bluegill for the same reasons.

Common carp, **buffalo**, and **suckers** compete with small bass and bluegill. They also destroy bass and bluegill habitat and muddy the pond bottom.

Golden shiners may become a problem also. They're excellent forage for bass, however, they compete with bluegill for food. In addition, they eat bluegill eggs.

HOW MANY AND WHEN

The rate and timing of fish stocking depends on your climate and fertilization techniques. (See "Fertilizing.")

Here are general guidelines that fit the majority of the pond community. *Rates are per surface acre and for fertilized ponds.*

If you do not add fertilizer, the stocking rate is usually half of that shown.

Stocking Fertilized Ponds October — March		
Fish	No.	Amount
Bluegill	1,000	2"-3"
or Bluegill/	800	
shellcracker	200	2"-3"
Fathead minnows	1,000	1"-2"
Grass carp	3-15	3"-4"
June		
Largemouth bass	100	3"-4"

In areas where bass grow more slowly, you might consider introducing advanced bass fingerlings (6 to 8 inches).

This can effectively reduce the time

In most states, public hatcheries deliver fingerlings to you at a central location in your area and advise you on the proper techniques for introducing the fish to their new home.

from stocking to fishing by nearly one year, compared with that which occurs with fingerling stocking programs.

WHERE AND HOW

In many states, bass, bream, and catfish are available from state fisheries. In others, hatchery fish go into public waters, and fish are not supplied to private pond owners.

If this is the case in your state, the list beginning on page 86 will provide a source that can point you toward reliable commercial hatcheries.

In states where fingerlings are furnished, ask your district fisheries biologist for an application or contact your county Extension agent. Plan to start the application process as early as possible.

Fish are distributed from public hatcheries from fall through spring in the order that applications are received. Although fish are available for several months, ponds that are stocked earlier in the fall are more likely to achieve balance.

Commercial hatcheries sell fish any time of year. However, you need to follow a set stocking schedule, either the one previously described or one that a consultant has set up to fit your fishing requirements.

An accurate estimate of your pond's surface acreage is necessary to determine the number and ratio of fish to stock. It may be time to refresh your memory about figuring pond dimensions. (See "Building: Determining Dimensions.")

If the surface area is overestimated, too many fish will be stocked for the available food supply and few will grow to a harvestable size.

If underestimated, there will be too much food and an incorrect ratio of predators-to-prey will become established, upsetting that important balance.

The hatchery personnel will give you instructions about containers to be used and procedures for transporting your fish.

Small fish can be stressed by sudden changes in water temperature. If there is more than a 5- to 10-degree difference between the temperature of the water in the container and your pond water, care needs to be taken in transferring the fish.

Once back at your pond, slowly add water from the pond to the container until the temperature is the same as the pond water before putting the fish in the pond.

BUILDING FISH ATTRACTORS

Old-time fishermen will tell you that you're likely to find the best fishing in spots where breaks in the bottom of a pond occur. Natural breaks include tree stumps, rock piles, or a point of land that juts into the pond.

Studies show that one reason there's good fishing in those places is that fish tend to orient themselves near solid objects. Also, some are drawn to spots where there's protected area for nesting. Other territorial fish like the seclusion of barriers in the open water.

Create fishing "hot spots" with rocks, logs, or bundles of brush.

Now if you built your pond according to our suggestions, you've got a good, clean bottom with no stumps to decay and allow possible leaks and no rusty tractor parts to injure swimmers' feet. So you're less likely to have natural attractors.

Aquatic plants fill the bill to some extent, and the dock you build to park your boat adds some structure. But to improve your fishing, it's a good idea to create artificial attractors for hiding places and gathering points for your fish population.

Too many escape areas may reduce your chances of catching enough fish to repay you for your effort and enough to keep the pond in balance. A rule of thumb would be one 10- x 15-foot attractor for every 2 to 3 acres of water.

It doesn't have to be an elaborate structure. Some of those large rocks you saved during construction can be put to good use to shelter fish. Before the pond

fills, arrange them so there are nooks and crannies between them for fish to navigate.

Earthen humps and islands work well also. These areas may be shallow enough to allow weeds to colonize, yet surrounded by deeper water to prevent their spreading.

Even brush that has been securely bundled and anchored with rocks or concrete blocks or slabs makes an inexpensive, effective attractor.

Here's one simple structure using easily found, long-last-

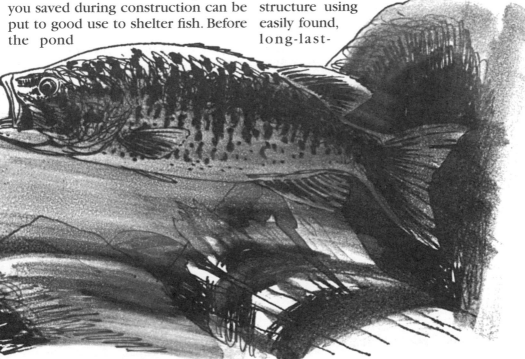

ing items: Punch holes in three old tires (so they'll sink), tie them together into a triangle, and weigh them down with cinder blocks.

A variation would be to forget the holes and fill one or more tires with concrete. Tying on some brush makes it even more appealing to the fish.

And get additional use out of your live Christmas tree. Drill a ⅜-inch hole at the base of the tree and push a steel bar or lag bolt into the hole. Put the tree in a 5-gallon can, filled three-quarters with concrete to hold it upright as well as to weigh it down.

Place the can on a hard, barren bottom in water less than 15 feet deep. If more than one tree is used, tie them together with polypropylene line.

Be sure to indicate the locations of the attractors somewhere on the shore or tie a marker to them so you'll easily find the fishing "hot spots."

Don't install fish attractors in navigable waters without a permit from the U.S. Army Corps of Engineers. And mark these attractors with permanent buoys.

FERTILIZING

There's good news and bad news about fertilizing fish ponds.

Supporters cite double benefits, and detractors point out the problems associated with improper application.

Fertilizing ponds has been shown to greatly enhance fish production. As we described earlier, the pond food chain begins with plankton and ends with healthy fish on your stringer. The practice of fertilizing is based on the idea of increasing plankton by adding nutrients.

A secondary benefit is in the control of aquatic growth. The "bloom" of the algae, which is encouraged by fertilization, will shade the pond bottom

Good fish management will ensure good catches of bream for your table.

and prevent weed growth.

The bloom is the growth of microscopic, or planktonic, algae that shows up in the green color of the water.

The downside of instituting a fertilization program is that this management strategy needs close attention. Appropriate timing and the amounts of fertilizer that are used determine your success.

Once you start adding nutrients, you have to continue. The increased fish population that has been created depends on this larger food supply. If you stop, the supply decreases down the line, and your fish won't have enough to eat.

And adding too many nutrients or adding them at the wrong time can create problems. The fertilizer could stimulate water weeds rather than plankton, if weeds already have an upper hand.

Adding it when the water is too cool will increase the amount of algae without creating the bloom.

Some specialists don't recommend fertilization. What has worked for pond owners around you will most likely be the best route for you to take. Talk to your county Extension agent, NRCS, or fisheries biologist about mud samples, water tests, and programs to fit your pond.

Many new ponds require a complete fertilizer, including nitrogen, phosphorus, and potassium.

Others may need only one or two of these nutrients. To keep fish growing and weeds in check, you need a plan that includes the right amounts of individual elements and the best time to add fertilizer.

A simple way to check the effectiveness of your fertilization efforts is to

---

So you'll have an idea of what is involved in a fertilization program, here are some general guidelines:

● Begin fertilizing when water surface temperature reaches 65° F.

● Use 1 gallon of 10-34-0 per surface acre every two weeks until bloom.

● The bloom should darken the water until it hides a white disk 20 inches below the surface.

● Continue fertilizing until the surface temperature drops below 65° F in the fall.

---

check the algae bloom. You can do this is by sticking a yardstick with a light-colored or shiny disk on the end straight down into the water. If you can see the object 18 inches or more in unmuddied water, you need to fertilize the pond.

Take note: Algae need sunlight and grow poorly in muddy water. If your pond is frequently muddy, you should control that problem first.

Visibility of less than 6 to 12 inches indicates super-abundant algae and a danger of oxygen depletion and fish kill in the pond. (See "Oxygen Depletion.")

The number of applications needed will vary from pond to pond. Those surrounded by fertilized lawns or pastures require fewer applications than those in wooded watersheds.

Detailed instructions for application usually are printed on the label. Liquid fertilizers must be spread over the entire surface, and some of them must be diluted before they're

applied.

Most liquid fertilizers are heavier than water. If they are poured at one spot, the nutrients sink to the bottom and become bound in sediments.

When applying granular fertilizers, keep the granules from contacting the bottom. If this happens, phosphorus becomes trapped and is unable to promote bloom development.

Here are several ways to apply granular fertilizer.

FROM THE BANK:
● If the pond is 1 to 3 acres in size, the fertilizer may be broadcast from the bank into the pond by going all the way around the water.

FROM A BOAT:
● Place a few short boards across the front end of the boat and put a sack of fertilizer on them.
● Let the fertilizer pour out in a thin stream while paddling or driving the boat around the edge in 3- to 4-foot deep water.
● There's no need to criss-cross the pond while applying the fertilizer. The winds will blow the top water in one direction, causing an undertow in the opposite direction.

FROM A PLATFORM:
● Construct a platform with a top that is 12 to 18 inches under the water. Build an above-water walkway to reach it from the bank.
● Tear off the top and sides of the sack and place it on the platform. The wind and waves will do the rest.
● Adjustment holes in the posts will allow the height to be changed for fluctuating water levels.

ON THE BOTTOM:
● Slit one of the flat sides of the bag of fertilizer in the form of the letter "H".
● Peel flaps back.
● Lay the bag in shallow water (but not directly on the pond bottom), with the open side facing the surface.
● If several bags are used, spread them out as much as possible.

To be effective, fertilization needs to be continued in succeeding years, and your pond needs may change. Monitor those changes by keeping watch on algae growth and taking mud samples as necessary.

LIMING
If the pond water remains clear and does not respond to fertilization, the problem probably is alkalinity.

"Soft" acidic water is inefficient at converting fertilizer into available nutrients. As we said in "Building," acid soils are common in many areas. Liming after construction and before the pond fills is a first step in maintaining the appropriate water conditions for good fish production.

An alkalinity level of 20 to 25 ppm and a pH of 6.5 to 9.0 is desirable for optimal fertilization benefits.

Test kits available from pond suppliers will tell you whether you need to add lime, but they don't specify the quantity. For that, you'll need to send randomly collected mud samples, including mud from the deep end of the pond, to a soil-testing laboratory for analysis.

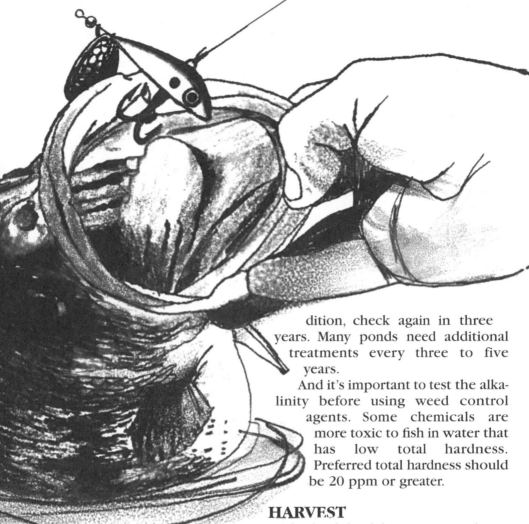

dition, check again in three years. Many ponds need additional treatments every three to five years.

And it's important to test the alkalinity before using weed control agents. Some chemicals are more toxic to fish in water that has low total hardness. Preferred total hardness should be 20 ppm or greater.

HARVEST

Think of the fish in your pond as a crop in which you've invested nutrients and management time and labor. Now you're ready for harvest. But unlike a crop, you don't see the complete results every year.

A successful yield is one that gives you a combination of sport and fun but leaves a fish population to grow in the pond for succeeding years.

Traditional fish management theory holds that many problems result from overharvesting bass. In recent years, however, pond consultants have found the opposite situation to be true. Not enough bass are harvested.

Spreading agricultural limestone across the pond surface is the preferred liming treatment. The rate of application usually varies from 2 to 5 tons per surface acre.

It takes three to four months to go into solution, and the finest grades (smallest particles) react the quickest. Coarse grades will be much slower to change the pH. The results of the lime application won't be immediately noticable in the pH measurement.

Liming doesn't require the constant monitoring that fertilization does. After you've corrected the initial con-

Bass-crowded ponds are characterized by an abundance of skinny, slow-growing bass, that measure in the 10- to 14-inch range. Lack of harvest allows the bass population to severely dampen bluegill numbers through intense predation.

As a result of this common problem, we suggest the following harvest program.

Fertilized ponds: After the first year, harvest bass up to 15 inches at a rate of 30 to 35 pounds per acre, per year. Bluegill should be removed only when they are desired for food.

Unfertilized ponds: Harvest bass up to 15 inches at a rate of 15 to 20 pounds per acre, per year. Again, only enough bluegill should taken out to fill your dinner plate.

In general, harvest may begin one year after the bass are stocked. The original stock (100 per acre), as well as larger fish (15 inches or more), may be protected if trophy bass production is an objective.

The size of your pond and your management program will determine its "carrying capacity," the number of pounds of fish it can support.

During the first year of fishing, a fertilized pond would yield 80 pounds of harvestable bream (about 320 fish) and 20 pounds of bass (15 to 20 fish) per surface acre.

In following years, it should produce 150 to 160 pounds of harvestable bream (600 to 700 fish) and 30 to 35 pounds of harvestable bass (25 to 30 fish) per surface acre, per year.

An unfertilized pond produces about 40 pounds of harvestable bream (about 120 fish) and 15 to 20 pounds of harvestable bass (12 to 15 fish) per surface acre, per year.

Spread out the fish harvest as long as possible.

BALANCE

The best way to monitor your fish population is to keep records on how many pounds of fish and what kinds are harvested.

A common complaint is that the bass/bluegill (bream) ratio is out of balance. We talked about too many bass in "Harvesting." When there are too many bream, the bass are no longer able to prevent them from eating bass eggs. Consequently, the bass population decreases even more.

Also, when there are too many bream, they don't grow very large because there is not enough food to go around.

You really can't get a completely accurate profile of the fish population unless trained biologists seine or electrofish the pond.

But a look at what you're pulling in can give you some clues.

So, and here's the best management technique we've mentioned so far, grab your rod and hit the water. That's one suggestion we probably don't have to repeat.

By fishing frequently, you can determine fish size and reproduction rate, and you can find out if any unwanted fish have slipped in. You'll also capture those older, larger fish before they succumb to natural mortality.

OK, you've had your fun. Now put down your rod and pick up a pencil. To ensure continued fishing success, you need to record your catch.

Ask any others who fish your pond to do the same. Also, make them aware of any limits that should be observed.

If you know the age and growth rate of fish in your pond, you'll be better able to diagnose and correct problems.

Review your catch records while keeping the following questions in mind.

● Is the average size of bluegill declining?

● Is the largest size of bluegill you catch getting smaller?

● Do you catch fewer big fish per hour or more little fish per hour?

● Are bass more difficult to catch?

● Are crappie, common carp, or other non-stocked fish showing up in the catch?

These notations will help you determine what kind of additional management, if any, is needed.

You also could drag a minnow seine, about 12 feet long and 4 feet deep. through shallow shoreline areas to sample your fish population.

Seining is especially effective in catching small bass and will aid you in determining how successfully the bass

Take a sample census of your underwater fish population by recording your catch.

are reproducing.

Report your findings to a pond or fisheries consultant, so he can suggest appropriate remedies.

RENOVATION

There may come a time when you've found that your fish population is seriously out of balance. The bass have disappeared, and the pond is overcrowded with stunted bluegills or trash fish like shad, bullheads, crappie, or suckers.

When this happens, the fishing is ruined, and it's time to make a tough decision. To re-establish a viable fish population, the existing fish must be eliminated and new ones stocked.

Kill out the fish population by draining the pond or by applying a fish toxicant.

Draining is the least expensive method, if you included a drain during construction. You also could invite all your friends to net fish and keep the good ones, as the water is lowered and they become concentrated.

If the pond can't be drained completely, look into poisoning. The most commonly used fish poison is rotenone, a natural substance found in the

stems and roots of certain tropical plants. Extracted from the dried roots, it is sold under a number of brand names and is widely available and inexpensive.

Rotenone has been used as a garden insecticide to control chewing insects, as a dust on cattle, or in dips for dogs and sheep, in addition to its role as a fish control agent. The common assumption is that rotenone "suffocates" fish. Actually, it inhibits a biochemical process that makes it impossible for fish to use oxygen in the release of energy needed for body processes.

Because rotenone breaks down into carbon dioxide and water after exposure to light, heat, oxygen, and alka-

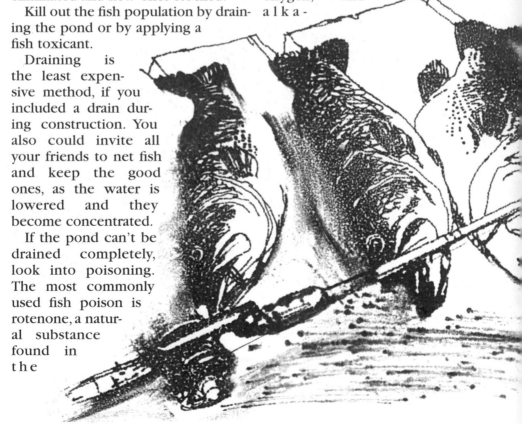

line water, it isn't considered a threat to animal or human health.

Calculations suggest that a 132-pound person would have to consume 535 pounds of raw fish containing 100 parts per billion of rotenone to acquire a toxic dose. But because the EPA has not set a tolerance of the substance, eating rotenone-killed fish is not recommended.

To ensure that the poison stays in the pond, there should be no water flowing when you treat it. If there's any danger of spillway overflows because of heavy rains, draw down the water before treatment.

The best time to apply rotenone is in early fall, so the pond can be restocked while hatchery fish are available. Toxicity is greatest when the temperature is between 50 and 70° F.

State regulations vary as to the application of rotenone. Check with your state fishery expert about any permits that may be required.

Treatments range from 0.5 parts per million to 5.0 ppm of the commercial products (5% formulations). The typical treatment rate is 2 ppm. The actual amount of rotenone involved in a 0.5 ppm treatment would be 25 parts per billion active ingredient; at 5 ppm, it would be 250 ppb.

Rotenone usually is diluted and applied through drip stations or sprayers or pumped

A healthy catch depends on good water quality.

through a hose into the propeller wash of a power boat. It also can be sprayed from the air.

The length of time it takes for rotenone to break down depends on temperature, light, oxygen, and alkalinity.

Detoxification will take four to five days if the water temperature is around 70° F. At 45° F, it may take 33 days.

Most ponds will be completely detoxified within 5 weeks. Before restocking, test the water by placing a small cage containing a few fish in the treated water. If you still have live fish after several days, it's safe to begin restocking. (Retrace your steps to "Stocking.")

KEEPING THE HABITAT HEALTHY

Once your fish are in residence, you have a few landlord duties to fulfill. Since the only way your tenants have of letting you know that something's wrong with the plumbing, heat, or air is to go belly up, it's up to you to watch out for potential breakdowns in the habitat.

OXYGEN DEPLETION

The amount of oxygen in your pond water is crucial. You need 4 to 5 ppm of dissolved oxygen for best management.

When levels are reduced, fish are stressed and more susceptible to disease. Depletion of dissolved oxygen is a common cause of fish kills.

The balance between oxygen production and demand can result from a number of situations: Too many fish, decomposition of organic matter (as a consequence of excessive fertilization

or herbicide use), and failure to produce enough oxygen through photosynthesis.

Seasonal changes affect oxygen levels. Certain climatic conditions can cause a sudden mixing of the layers, or a "turnover." This usually occurs in the spring and fall.

Pond water generally has three levels. The top layer is the productive layer. It contains most of the oxygen-producing phytoplankton. The middle is a thin mixing layer characterized by sudden drops in temperature and dissolved oxygen concentrations. And the bottom layer is made up of the coldest and heaviest water, with little oxygen.

Cold, severe rains put a layer of cold water on top, forcing warm water to the bottom and mixing the layers. If there isn't enough oxygen in the upper layer to maintain sufficient levels throughout the mixed water column, oxygen depletion and fish kills can occur.

In the summer, warm water holds less dissolved oxygen, and dangerously low levels can occur. The natural summertime evaporation of water from feeder springs and streams and from the pond itself, coupled with decaying vegetation because of herbicide treatments, points to a potential disaster.

Too much cloudy weather anytime, as well as heavy snow and ice cover in winter, also can promote oxygen depletion. Several consecutive days without sunlight can cause aquatic plants to produce less oxygen than fish consume.

During any situation except the ice conditions described above, watch the behavior of your fish for signs of potential oxygen depletion.

1. Fish will swim to surface and gulp air. If disturbed, they dive but quickly return to the surface. Early morning is the best time to check.

2. Fish may surface in the early morning but return to deeper water as dissolved oxygen builds up during the day.

Better yet, monitor oxygen levels during critical times. Test kits are available that range in price from under $50 for liquid sample tests to several hundred dollars for electronic meters.

If snow is the problem, prevent fish kills by removing snow from at least 50% of the pond surface. Drilling holes in the ice will not help.

Reduce the possibility of summer kills by making sure no fertilizer, herbicides, insecticides, or organic runoff (silage, manure) enter the pond. Restrict herbicide treatments to selected areas in late July and August to prevent excessive decaying vegetation.

AERATION

When the natural actions of wind, rain, and photosynthesis do not contribute adequate oxygen, fish become stressed and fish kills are likely to occur.

Aeration is the process of using motor-driven air compressors or wind-driven baffles to increase the dissolved oxygen in the pond water.

Aerators also are used sometimes to increase fish productivity. Once this

A paddle-wheel aerator moves large volumes of water with the least amount of energy expended.

process is initiated as a management strategy, however, it must be continued.

Aeration increases production by destratifying the pond and increasing the productive area. Normally, fish production is in the upper third of the pond. When oxygen is moved through all levels by aeration, you can increase the productive area.

If you stop aeration, the pond layers will stratify again, and there won't be sufficient oxygen available. This is particularly a problem during warm weather.

There are a number of ways that the water can be aerated mechanically. Local pond equipment dealers can advise you about the size and type of equipment that will be right for your pond.

When signs of oxygen depletion are noted, the sooner an aerator is used and the larger the volume of water sprayed or agitated, the more effective it will be. Also, it is important not to disturb the bottom mud.

Try these quick fixes: 1) Use an irrigation pump to force water into the air, letting it splash back into the pond. 2) Add 100 pounds of triple superphosphate per surface acre. If fish are having difficulty breathing or appear to be dying the second morning, make another application. 3) Add 1 pound of potassium permanganate for each 200 linear feet of shoreline. This is a fungicide, but it has been used to relieve oxygen deficiency.

Pumps and aerator attachments for tractor PTO's often don't produce enough oxygenated water to prevent a fish kill because the devices aren't powerful enough. For a 5-acre pond, you'll need a 5 hp aerator, 1 hp for each surface acre.

Fish will flock to the newly oxygenated water, but there won't be enough produced to save the pond.

The same goes for the fountains and waterfalls that designers add to serve double duty. They are attractive additions to the water area, but most often their power is not adequate to alleviate oxygen-short conditions.

Other aerators offer long-term, effective service, if properly chosen and installed. **Surface aerators**, like the paddle-wheel, operate much like a miniature waterfall. A propeller close to the water level splashes water into the air. As it falls back into the pond, the water is oxygenated. Some surface splashers float on the water, and some are installed on rigid posts in the water.

The cost of operating a surface aerator depends on the oxygen requirements, the size of the pond, the power of the unit, and the frequency of use.

If the aerator is operated by an electrical hookup in the water, special care must be taken to fuse the line to prevent accidental short circuits. For people who want to enjoy swimming as well as raising fish, it would be prudent to disconnect the splasher when in the water.

A **diffusion aerator** oxygenates the water from below the surface. A compressor on shore pumps air through flexible tubing to an underwater diffuser on the pond bottom. Air bubbles float up to the surface and thus oxygenate the water.

To be effective, a diffuser should be set up at a depth of at least 4 to 5 feet to ensure adequate "hang time" as the bubbles rise and give off oxygen. Diffusers use less power than surface splashers.

Pond owners especially like diffusers because there is no electrical hookup to run in the water and no mooring lines to tangle up boats and swimmers.

Diffusers require maintenance to keep the venting holes clean. Slime will accumulate on the diffuser and cause back pressure on the compressor. A gauge can be installed on the compressor to monitor pressure.

CLEARING MUDDY WATER

Some causes of muddy water were mentioned in "Building." Besides creating unwanted sediment deposits, muddy water can reduce the food and oxygen supply and irritate fish gills. Fish under stress are more susceptible to diseases, and reproduction is decreased.

Mud also prevents sunlight from penetrating the water. This reduces the growth of phytoplankton, the first link in the pond's food chain.

One study showed that 28-month-old bass in five experimental clear ponds weighed almost five times as much as bass of the same age in five muddy ponds.

Sediments washed into ponds after heavy rains will change pond color. But color should return to normal within a few days or weeks as settling occurs. If it doesn't, corrective measures need to be taken for the watershed. (See "Decreasing Silt.")

Probably the simplest and most useful method for improving muddy water conditions is liming. Solids tend to remain in solution longer in acidic water. Increasing the alkalinity and pH by liming tends to "clear" the water of suspended solids.

Muddy water can sometimes be corrected by spreading broken bales of high quality hay around the shoreline. As the hay decays, a weak acid is formed that causes clay particles to settle.

About 5 bales of hay per surface acre is recommended. However, don't do this in hot weather or you could cause severe oxygen depletion.

Other methods include adding gypsum (land plaster), commercial alum crystals, or cottonseed meal. And, in mild cases, standard fertilization procedures can help.

If muddy water is caused by common carp or bullheads, complete pond draining or chemical eradication may be warranted.

PARASITES AND DISEASES

Fish are exposed to a wide range of diseases and parasites, and it's normal to see a few dead fish from time to time. But serious losses of fish because of disease or parasites are unusual in a natural environment.

If you have a large fish kill, look for other sources, including oxygen depletion or water contamination.

The angler who is concerned about eating affected fish needs to keep in mind a thought from fishing experts: A sick fish is not going to bite the hook.

Humans are not likely to suffer ill effects from consuming fish that have been thoroughly cleaned, including the removal of any unappetizing flesh, before cooking. If you have any doubt, though, don't eat the fish.

Your initial job in ensuring the good health of your fish population is to get your supply from a reputable hatchery. Then, your management techniques can affect their continued health.

Unfavorable water quality can speed the development of organisms that already exist in the fish environment.

Symptoms vary according to the fish species, but these are general indications of the presence of disease or parasites.

External

● *Bacteria:* Lesions, sores, hemorrhages, pop-eyed, blood under scales, or loss of scales.

● *Fungus:* Cotton-like, white-tan-grey fuzzy growth on body or fins.

● *Ich:* Small, pinhead-sized white spots on the skin of catfish and sometimes excessive mucus production.

● *Black spot:* Small, black-to-purple spots under the skin or in the flesh of scale fish.

● *Eye flukes:* Eye opaque or deformed.

● *Gill parasites:* Gills swollen and pink.

● *Roundworms:* Thread-like red worm extending from the anus.

● *Leeches:* Worm-like animal attached to the body, head, fins, or gills or a circular wound left by one.

● *Anchor worm:* Small, red pustual with red threadlike body protruding from wound at the base of scale or on or near the base of fins.

● *Fish louse:* Small, bloody areas at the base or under the scales of a fish.

Internal

● *Flukes, tapeworms, roundworms, spiny-headed worms:* White worms in the intestine.

● *Tapeworm:* Large, white flat worm in body cavity.

● *Larval roundworm:* Worm in cyst on internal organs, coiled like a watch spring.

● *Larval flukes:* Small cysts on internal organs.

● *Larval tapeworms:* Small, white threadlike worms on or in internal organs.

● *Spiny-headed worm:* Small, white-to-orange worm in body cavity or attached to intestines.

If oxygen levels drop, fish are stressed and are more susceptible to bacterial infections. Spring die-offs often are the results of a reduction of oxygen, coupled with frenzied spawning activity that further strains the fish.

A FISHPOND FOR ALL SEASONS

October: Complete pond construction and begin stocking with bluegill, redear, and catfish. If the pond was completed earlier and has received water that might contain wild fish, it must be drained and poisoned before stocking.

Feed bluegill during October and November when water temperatures range between 60 and 80° F to increase the number and size of the fish. Collect mud samples so you can add lime as needed.

November: Apply lime according to mud test results when fertilization has been stopped. This gives lime a chance to react with the acid bottom muds before spring application of fertilizer.

If weeds are a problem, drain water so that at least half of the pond bottom is exposed from November through February.

Drawdowns also concentrate the fish, making forage fish more available to bass, increasing bass growth and reducing bream. Don't reduce water level in ponds smaller than 1 acre. If shallow water plants are a big problem, deepen pond edges while the water is down.

February: In some parts of the country, you can start your fertilizer program now, adding more at recom-

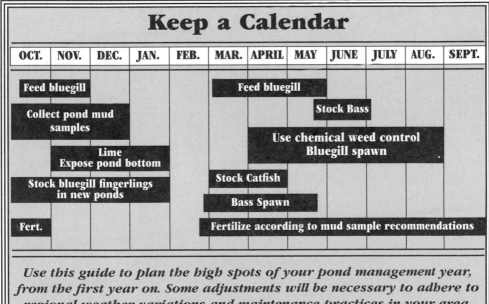

Keep a Calendar

OCT.	NOV.	DEC.	JAN.	FEB.	MAR.	APRIL	MAY	JUNE	JULY	AUG.	SEPT.

Feed bluegill

Feed bluegill

Collect pond mud samples

Stock Bass

Use chemical weed control
Bluegill spawn

Lime
Expose pond bottom

Stock Catfish

Stock bluegill fingerlings in new ponds

Bass Spawn

Fert.

Fertilize according to mud sample recommendations

Use this guide to plan the high spots of your pond management year, from the first year on. Some adjustments will be necessary to adhere to regional weather variations and maintenance practices in your area.

mended rates at set intervals through October. Check with your state fisheries consultant to get the appropriate time and rates for your area.

March: Start a spring feeding program for bluegill. In some areas, this is continued through the summer.

Stock catfish during March and April, but be sure they're more than 8 inches long if bass are in the pond. This also is a good time to stock grass carp for weed control. The size you need depends on the other fish in the pond.

April: The best time to control water weeds with herbicides is before they reach maturity. Follow instructions on the label. Harvest bluegill and redear.

May: Stock small bass late in the month and in June. Check the balance of bluegill and bass by seining from May through September. A pond consultant or fisheries biologist can give you a good idea of the health of your pond from the results of the balance check.

June: Begin fishing new ponds one year after bass have been stocked.

July, August, September: Enjoy catching fish. Continue herbicide weed control and discontinue fertilization if weeds have gotten out of hand.

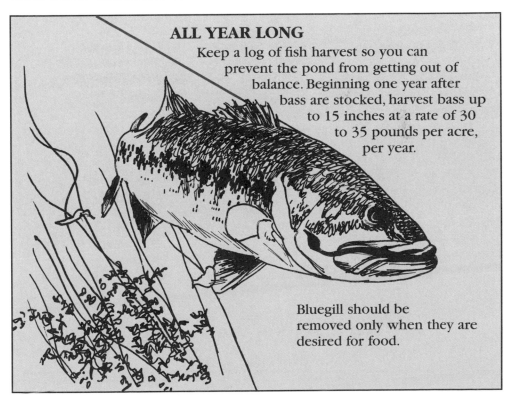

ALL YEAR LONG

Keep a log of fish harvest so you can prevent the pond from getting out of balance. Beginning one year after bass are stocked, harvest bass up to 15 inches at a rate of 30 to 35 pounds per acre, per year.

Bluegill should be removed only when they are desired for food.

Enjoying Your Water Paradise

Points to Pond-er

▶ Read "Building" again so you'll have fewer problems and more free time.

▶ Think safety for swimming and boating.

▶ Keep structures in good repair.

▶ Have fun at your pond.

III.
ENJOYING

All right now, admit it. Your first thought when you envisioned a pond wasn't about all that extra water you'd have for fighting fires or watering livestock.

And most likely, taking care of the wilting cabbages in the garden didn't take the top spot either.

No, more likely, it was the idea that come that first spring-like day, you could grab your fishing rod, slide your boat into the still-cool water, and cast for that big bass.

Or you pictured yourself presiding over the family barbecue on the Fourth of July and your kids splashing away the summer heat right at home.

You aren't alone. For many pond owners, enjoyment is a prime motivation for the time and money spent on adding a pond to their place.

We couldn't wrap up our book without including several ideas that will help you enjoy yourself. Included in this section are safety and fishing tips, as well as plans for a picnic table and a screened building for a barbecue pit to add to your outdoor fun.

To make your winged friends happy, we're also giving you a plan for a wood duck nest box.

And as we said up front, with planning and effort, you can have your own pond: Come on in, the water's fine.

SAFETY FIRST

It goes without saying that you don't want your water fun to turn into tragedy. But there's an additional reason for a focus on safety.

Give this statistic some consideration: In the past 25 years, water-related activities have generated the largest number of recreational-accident lawsuits. The following suggestions can help protect your family and also lessen your liability.

Swimming

As soon as you decide that swimming will be one of the activities at your pond, outline the spot with buoys and ropes. This will define the safe area and protect boaters from shallow water.

Include the following in your plans and practices:

1. Make the swimming area no more than 4 feet deep, with no drop-offs and no rocks underfoot. And as we said earlier, remove all stumps during construction.

2. Mark diving places and make sure the water is at least 8 feet deep.

3. Provide safe access into and out of the water, no steep banks.

4. Keep rescue equipment handy, including ring buoys, ropes, or long

poles. Instruct all swimmers about where and how to use them.
5. Don't allow anyone to swim alone, after dark, or during electrical storms.
6. Use the buddy system in which two swimmers are designated to watch out for each other.

Boating
1. Provide Coast Guard-approved flotation devices and insist that all aboard use them.
2. Prohibit dangerous horseplay.
3. Be sure that anyone operating a motor-driven boat or even paddling a canoe knows what they're doing and can be responsible for their passengers.
4. If possible, lock boats and store them away from the water when not in use.

All Around
1. Keep docks, piers, and any other pond-side structures in good condition.

2. Remove rundown buildings or platforms you don't intend to upgrade.
3. Elevate electrical lines you install for floodlights or bug zappers out of the reach of fishing rods and watch lines for signs of fraying.
4. Fence the pond and keep the gate locked when you aren't using it.

FISHING FACTS

Keep Fish Fresh From the Hook to the Cook

■ For stringers: Try to use the safety-pin type, string only one fish per link, and string it through the lower lip.
■ Wire basket: Don't crowd fish or put in dead fish.
■ Stringers and wire baskets: Remove these from the water when moving the boat. Fish die quickly when water is forced through the gills.
■ For waders: Use an old-fashioned wicker or canvas creel so that air flows around fish. Don't allow water to sit inside.
■ As soon as possible, clean, remove

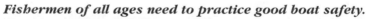

Fishermen of all ages need to practice good boat safety.

Your investment in a well-built pond will allow you and your family many years of enjoyment.

gills and entrails, and dry fish with a paper towel.

■ If you can't have a shore lunch, pack fish in a zip-top plastic bag in an ice chest. Use ice cubes or chips to surround the fish, rather than blocks to sit them on.

■ When you don't plan to eat your catch right away, freeze the fish in a block of ice to seal the flesh from outside air. A clean milk carton, lightly packed with fish, and filled up to ½ inch

of the top makes a good container. Fish frozen this way usually are good up to six months.

■ When you have no way to store fish properly, practice catch and release. It's the responsible thing to do.

Raise Your Own Bait

10 steps to growing crickets

Crickets make good bait for bluegill and catfish. They're most abundant in May, June, and late fall and usually can be found under piles of decaying plants. But you can have your own supply in a month, any time of year, as long as you maintain the appropriate temperature.

1. Catch crickets outdoors or buy them from a commercial dealer.

2. Provide a brood pen with protection from ants, spiders, and other parasites.

3. Make a pen out of a metal can (garbage can, lard can, metal drum without top) with a minimum depth of 18 to 24 inches and as wide as possible. Set it on legs, and place each leg in a large can of water or oil. If it's a large pen, screen the top to keep crickets from jumping out and to prevent other animals or insects from getting in.

4. Clean the inside of pen thoroughly and sand sides smoothly with fine sandpaper 8 to 10 inches from the top. Apply two coats of a good grade of floor wax to this area, polishing between coats with cheesecloth.

5. Put in 4 to 6 inches of clean, fine, moist sand. It must stay moist for crickets to lay eggs.

6. The sand needs to be relatively dry while young crickets are growing. Moisten again in about three months. By that time. the young crickets have matured and are ready to lay eggs.

7. Place 4 to 5 inches of wood excelsior over the sand. In the center, put a

Fish With a Chum

Nothing works better at hooking kids on fishing than catching something the first time out. Take a can of fish-flavored cat food with you to the fishing hole.

Punch a few holes in the sides and bottom, tie the can to a length of line, and sink it off the side of the boat or dock.

The fish will be attracted to the chum and stay around longer.

glass jar drinking fountain similar to one for watering baby chicks, with cotton filling the saucer slightly above the water level. That will allow crickets to get water without drowning. Replenish the supply, clean the saucer, and replace the cotton every four to six weeks.

8. Chicken laying mash is excellent feed. Place it in a saucer and press it down into the excelsior.

9. Allow 2 square feet of rearing space for each 20 to 30 adults, with a male-female ratio of 50-50. Identify the females by the long tube at the rear end that deposits eggs.

10. Keep the pen where the temperature is between 80 and 90° F while they're growing. As soon as the crickets reach bait size, reduce the heat so growth slows.

Fiddle for worms

It's almost a lost art, but old-time fishermen swear by it. Drive a pole 6 to 8 inches into the ground, depending on the soil moisture. After it's set, move a saw back and forth across the top, making the teeth go deep enough into the stick to cause it to vibrate.

Some say the worms pop out of the ground because they can't stand the vibrations; others insist they're trying to escape the moles that they think are digging for their dinner.

A tree full of fish bait

The catalpa worm is considered a top bait for bluegills. It's the larva of

the sphinx moth, which lays its eggs on catalpa trees, and the first hatch usually appears in June.

The trees, also known as a cigar tree and an Indian bean tree, are available from many state tree nurseries.

Angling Asides

And we'll close on these words of wisdom from fishermen through the ages:

A fishing line has a hook at one end and an optimist at the other.

❀

It's good to be at the top of the food chain.

❀

There's no such thing as too much equipment.

❀

Even the best lines get weak after they've been used a few times.

Planning for Friends
Picnic Table and Benches

Here's a sturdy, easy-to-build picnic table that will last through countless picnics and fish cleanings.

The table is 6 feet long and 28 inches wide, a convenient size for six people.

The table legs shown are 37 inches long, so the height of the table is 28 inches. If you have tall people in the family, you may want to make leg pieces an inch or two longer. Also increase the

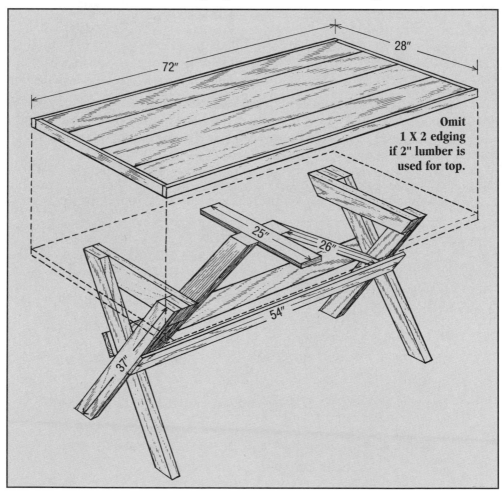

72"

28"

Omit
1 X 2 edging
if 2" lumber is
used for top.

25"

26"

54"

37"

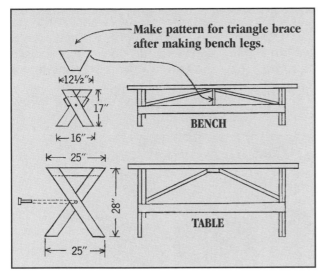

Make pattern for triangle brace after making bench legs.

12½"

17"

16"

BENCH

25"

28"

25"

TABLE

height of the benches to conform.

Except for the 1x2 molding around the top of the table, both benches and the table can be built of 1x4's. This is suitable for normal family use. For rugged duty, use 2-inch lumber.

The diagonal braces on the benches and table and the triangular braces on the benches are essential to the construction. Use either nails or screws.

Screened Barbecue Pit

There's nothing like an old-fashioned barbecue pit if you're cooking for a crowd. Add a roof for shade and screening to keep out flies, and you have the makings for a fine cookout.

This pit can be built in increments

of 5 feet, from 5 to 30 feet long. The concrete slab and the roof extend past both ends of the pit to allow free movement around the entire pit.

Metal doors at either end of the pit give convenient access to the firebox. The plans include an adjustable grill that allows slow or fast cooking of meat. This cooking area is a good spot to install a water outlet to allow speedy cleanup.

Note that screening the pit requires two additional posts at front and back that are not shown on the drawing.

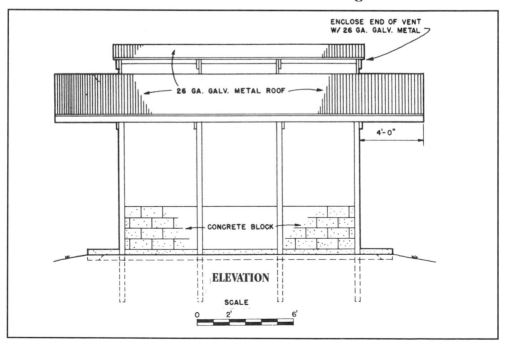

ENCLOSE END OF VENT W/ 26 GA. GALV. METAL

26 GA. GALV. METAL ROOF

4'-0"

CONCRETE BLOCK

ELEVATION

SCALE

0   2'   6'

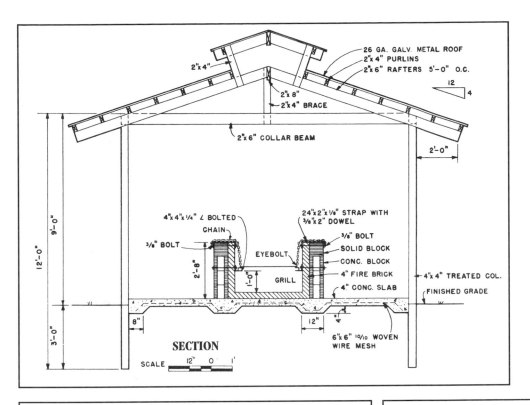

26 GA. GALV. METAL ROOF
2"x 4" PURLINS
2"x 6" RAFTERS 5'-0" O.C.

2"x 4"

2"x 8"
2"x 4" BRACE

2"x 6" COLLAR BEAM

12
4

2'-0"

4"x 4"x 1/4" ∠ BOLTED

24"x 2"x 1/8" STRAP WITH
3/8"x 2" DOWEL

CHAIN

3/8" BOLT

3/8" BOLT
SOLID BLOCK
CONC. BLOCK

EYEBOLT

GRILL

4" FIRE BRICK
4" CONC. SLAB

4"x 4" TREATED COL.

FINISHED GRADE

9'-0"

12'-0"

2'-8"

1'-0"

3'-0"

8"

12"

6"x 6" 10/10 WOVEN
WIRE MESH

SECTION

SCALE   12"   O   1'

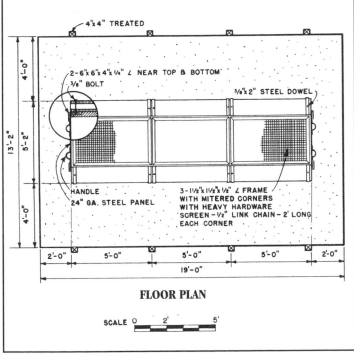

4"x 4" TREATED

2-6"x 6"x 4"x 1/4" ∠ NEAR TOP & BOTTOM

3/8" BOLT

3/8"x 2" STEEL DOWEL

4'-0"

5'-2"

13'-2"

4'-0"

HANDLE

24" GA. STEEL PANEL

3-11/2"x 11/2"x 1/2" ∠ FRAME
WITH MITERED CORNERS
WITH HEAVY HARDWARE
SCREEN - 1/2" LINK CHAIN - 2' LONG
EACH CORNER

2'-0"   5'-0"   5'-0"   5'-0"   2'-0"

19'-0"

FLOOR PLAN

SCALE   O   2'   5'

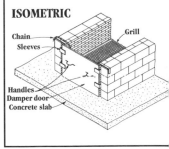

ISOMETRIC

Chain
Sleeves

Grill

Handles
Damper door
Concrete slab

Wood Duck Nest Box

If you'd like wood ducks to share your pond, you'll go a long way toward attracting them with this nesting box.

Wood ducks are different from other ducks. They like to land and perch in trees, and they like a nest off the ground. The first requirement is a shallow marsh area with some standing cover that will provide seed and insects for food and that will serve as a hiding place for ducklings.

Dead standing and fallen trees make good natural nesting areas, but you're not likely to have those around your new pond. This simple box has been used with great success in many areas of the country.

The way the box is built and mounted will determine whether ducks use it and how safe the eggs and babies will be inside.

1. The size of the entrance hole is critical. An oblong hole 3 inches tall and 4 inches wide is fine for the hen and will discourage owls. It also keeps out larger raccoons, one of the wood duck's worst enemies.

2. Use unplaned, untreated cedar, cypress, or other weather-resistant lumber.

3. You'll need a 4-inch strip of metal hardware cloth on the inside front, from the bottom of the box to the opening, so the ducklings can climb out of the box.

4. It needs to be mounted at least 5 to 6 feet above the water level, but 10 feet is ideal. Mounting the nest box over the water helps keep out most predators, but we've included a guard on this plan.

5. Place the boxes where they'll be shaded but are not close to overhanging limbs that snakes can use for access. And mount them facing open areas so woodies in search of cavities will see them.

6. Mount the boxes before the season comes. Clean the box every year and put in at least 3 inches of clean wood shavings or hay.

7. Wood ducks will tolerate close nesting, so several boxes can be mounted on the same pole or close to each other. Being fairly close to your house also won't bother them.

Don't expect full use of your boxes the first year. Birds can take several seasons to get used to them, but the rate goes up by the second or third year. Birds that hatched and came out of a box will more readily use one.

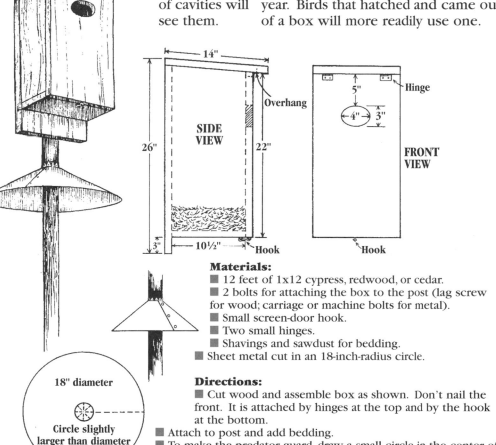

Materials:
- 12 feet of 1x12 cypress, redwood, or cedar.
- 2 bolts for attaching the box to the post (lag screw for wood; carriage or machine bolts for metal).
- Small screen-door hook.
- Two small hinges.
- Shavings and sawdust for bedding.
- Sheet metal cut in an 18-inch-radius circle.

Directions:
- Cut wood and assemble box as shown. Don't nail the front. It is attached by hinges at the top and by the hook at the bottom.
- Attach to post and add bedding.
- To make the predator guard, draw a small circle in the center of the sheet metal slightly larger than the diameter of the support post. Cut from the edge of the metal to the center point. Then make a series of short cuts from the center to the small circle. Bend the tabs up and wrap the predator guard around the post. Rivet or bolt the overlapping metal edges to form a cone and then attach the cone to the post with nails or sheet-metal screws.

Where To Get Help
USDA-NRCS STATE CONSERVATION OFFICES

■ **Alabama**
665 Opelika Rd.
Auburn, AL 36830
334-887-4506

■ **Alaska**
949 E. 36th
Suite 400
Anchorage, AK 99508-4362
907-271-2424

■ **Arizona**
3003 N. Central
Suite 800
Phoenix, AZ 85012-2945
602-280-8808

■ **Arkansas**
Federal Bldg., Room 5804
700 W. Capitol
Little Rock, AR 72201
501-324-5648

■ **California**
2121-C 2nd St.
Davis, CA 95616
916-757-8262

■ **Caribbean Area**
150 Cardon Ave.
Federal Bldg.
Hato Rey, PR 00918
809-766-5206

■ **Colorado**
655 Parfet St.
Room E200C
Lakewood, CO 80215-5517
303-236-2886

■ **Connecticut**
16 Professional Park Rd.
Storrs, CT 06268-1299
860-487-4013

■ **Delaware**
Suite 101
1203 College Park Dr.
Dover, DE 19904-8713
302-678-4160

■ **Florida**
P.O. Box 141510
2614 NW 43rd St.
Gainesville, FL 32614-1510
904-338-9500

■ **Georgia**
Federal Bldg., Box 13
355 E. Hancock
Athens, GA 30601
706-546-2272

Hawaii
Federal Bldg.
300 Ala Moana Blvd.
Honolulu, HI 96850
808-541-2605

Idaho
3244 Elder
Room 1241
Boise, ID 83705
208-334-1601

Illinois
1902 Fox Dr.
Champaign, IL 61820
217-398-5267

Indiana
6013 Lakeside Dr.
Indianapolis, IN 46278-2933
317-290-3200

Iowa
693 Federal Bldg.
210 Walnut St.
Des Moines, IA 50309
515-284-4261

Kansas
760 S. Broadway
Salina, KS 67401
913-823-4565

Kentucky
771 Corporate, #110
Lexington, KY 40503
606-224-7350

Louisiana
3737 Government St.
Alexandria, LA 71302
318-473-7751

Maine
5 Godfrey Dr.
Orono, ME 04473
207-866-7245

Maryland
339 Busch's Frontage Rd.
Suite 301
Annapolis, MD 21401
410-757-0861

Massachusetts
451 West St.
Amherst, MA 01002
413-253-4351

Michigan
1405 S. Harrison Rd.
Room 101
East Lansing, MI 48823-5202
517-337-6701

Minnesota
600 Farm Credit Bldg.
375 Jackson St.
St. Paul, MN 55101-1854
612-290-3675

Mississippi
McCoy Federal Bldg.
100 W. Capitol St.
Jackson, MS 39269-1399
601-965-5205

Missouri
601 Business Loop 70 W.
Parkade Center, Suite 250
Columbia, MO 65203
314-876-0900

Montana
10 E. Babcock, Federal Bldg.
Bozeman, MT 59715-4704
406-587-6814

■ **Nebraska**
Federal Bldg., Room 152
100 Centennial Mall
Lincoln, NE 68508
402-437-5300

■ **Nevada**
Bldg. F, Suite 220
5301 Longley Lane
Reno, NV 89511
702-784-5863

■ **New Hampshire**
Federal Bldg.
Durham, NH 03824
603-868-7581

■ **New Jersey**
1370 Hamilton St.
Somerset, NJ 08873
908-246-1662

■ **New Mexico**
6200 Jefferson, NE
Albuquerque, NM 87109-3734
505-761-4400 & 4401

■ **New York**
441 South Salina St.
5th Floor, Suite 354
Syracuse, NY 13202-2450
315-477-6504

■ **North Carolina**
Somerset Park, Suite 205
4405 Bland, Somerset
Raleigh, NC 27609
919-790-2888

■ **North Dakota**
Rosser Ave. & Third
Bismarck, ND 58502
701-250-4421

■ **Ohio**
200 N. High St.
Columbus, OH 43215
614-469-6962

■ **Oklahoma**
100 USDA Ag. Bldg.
Suite 203
Stillwater, OK 74074-2655
405-742-1200

■ **Oregon**
101 SW Main, Suite 1300
Portland, OR 97204
503-414-3262

■ **Pennsylvania**
One Credit Union Pl.
Suite 340
Harrisburg, PA 17110
717-782-2202

■ **Rhode Island**
60 Quaker Lane, Suite 46
Warwick, RI 02886
401-828-1300

■ **South Carolina**
1835 Assembly, Federal Bldg.
Columbia, SC 29201
803-253-5681

■ **South Dakota**
Federal Bldg.
200 Fourth, SW
Huron, SD 57350-2475
605-352-1200

■ **Tennessee**
675 U.S. Courthouse
801 Broadway
Nashville, TN 37203
615-736-5471

■ **Texas**
101 S. Main
Poage Federal Bldg.
Temple, TX 76501-7682
817-774-1214

■ **Utah**
Federal Bldg., 125 S. State
Salt Lake City, UT 84147
801-524-5050

■ **Vermont**
69 Union St.
Winooski, VT 05404
802-951-6795

■ **Virginia**
400 N. 8th St., #209
1606 Santa Rosa Rd.
Richmond, VA 23229-5014
804-287-1691

■ **Washington**
W. 316 Boone Ave., Suite 450
Spokane, WA 99201-2348
509-353-2337

■ **West Virginia**
75 High St., Room 301
Morgantown, WV 26505
304-291-4484

■ **Wisconsin**
6515 Watts Rd.
Suite 200
Madison, WI 53719-2726
608-264-5341 ext. 122

■ **Wyoming**
Federal Bldg., Room 3124
100 East B St.
Casper, WY 82601
307-261-6453

■ **Pacific Basin**
FHB Bldg., Suite 301
400 Route 8
Maite, Guam 96927
8-700-550-7490

STATE FISHERY CHIEFS

■ **Alabama**
Fred Harders
Chief Division of Fisheries
AL Dept. of Conservation & Natural Resources
64 N. Union St.
Montgomery, AL 36130
334-242-3471
R. Vernon Minton
Director, Division of Marine Resources
AL Dept. of Conservation & Natural Resources
P.O. Box 189
Dauphin Island, AL 36528
334-861-2882

■ **Alaska**
John Burke
Division of Sport Fish
AK Dept. of Fish & Game
P.O. Box 25526
Juneau, AK 99802-5526
907-465-4180

■ **Arizona**
Joseph L. Janisch
Supervisor, Fisheries branch
AZ Game & Fish Dept.
2222 W. Greenway Rd.
Phoenix, AZ 85023
602-942-3000

■ **Arkansas**
F. Allen Carter
Chief, Division of Fisheries
AR Game & Fish Commission
#2 Natural Resources Dr.

Little Rock, AR 72205
501-223-6371

■ **California**
Tim Farley
Chief, Inland Fisheries Division
CA Dept. Fish & Game
CA Resources Agency
1416 Ninth St.
Sacramento, CA 95814
916-653-6194
L.B. Boydstun
Acting Chief, Marine Resources Division
CA Dept. Fish & Game
Marine Resources Agency
1416 Ninth St.
Sacramento, CA 95814
916-653-6281

■ **Colorado**
Ed Kochman
Manager, Aquatic Wildlife Section
State Aquatic Wildlife
CO Division of Wildlife
6060 Broadway
Denver, CO 80216
303-291-7356

■ **Connecticut**
James C. Moulton
Asst. Director
Inland Fisheries Division
79 Elm St.
Hartford, CT 06106
203-424-3474
Eric M. Smith
Assistant Director
Marine Fisheries Division

CT Dept. Environmental Protection
P.O. Box 719
Old Lyme, CT 06371
203-434-6043
■ **Delaware**
Andrew T. Manus
Director, Division Fish & Wildlife
DE DNR & Environmental Control
P.O. Box 1401
Dover, DE 19903
(89 Kings Hwy.)
302-739-5295
■ **Florida**
Dr. Jerome Shireman
Director, Division of Fisheries
FL Game & Fresh Water Fish
Commission
620 South Meridian St.
Tallahassee, FL 32399-1600
904-488-4676
Ed Conklin
Director, Division Marine Resources
FL Dept. Natural Resources
3900 Commonwealth Blvd.
Tallahassee, FL 32399
904-488-6058
■ **Georgia**
Richard M. Gennings
Chief, Fisheries Management
GA Dept. of Natural Resources
2070 U.S. Hwy. 278-SE
Social Circle, GA 30279
404-918-6400
Susan Shipman
Chief, Coastal Fisheries
GA Dept. of Natural Resources

1 Conservation Way
Brunswick, GA 31523-8600
912-264-7218
■ **Hawaii**
Division of Aquatic Resources
HI Dept. of Land & Natural
Resources
1151 Punchbowl St.
Honolulu, HI 96813
808-587-0100
■ **Idaho**
Steven M. Huffaker
Chief, Bureau of Fisheries
ID Fish & Game Dept.
600 S. Walnut, Box 25
Boise, ID 83707
208-334-3700
■ **Illinois**
Mike Conlin
Chief, Division of Fisheries
IL Dept. of Natural Resources
524 S. Second St.
Springfield, IL 62701-1787
217-782-6424
■ **Indiana**
William D. James
Chief of Fisheries
IN Dept. Natural Resources
402 E. Washington St. #W273
Indianapolis, IN 46204
317-232-4080

■ **Iowa**
Marion Conover
Chief, Fisheries Bureau
Fish & Wildlife Division
IA Dept. Natural Resources
Wallace State Office Bldg.
East Ninth & Grand Ave.
Des Moines, IA 50319
515-281-5918

■ **Kansas**
Joe Kramer
Chief, Fisheries & Wildlife Division
KS Dept. of Wildlife & Parks
512 SE 25th Ave.
Pratt, KS 67124-9599
316-672-5911 (191)

■ **Kentucky**
Peter W. Pfeiffer
Director, Division of Fisheries
KY Dept. of Fish & Wildlife
Resources
#1 Game Farm Rd.
Frankfort, KY 40601
502-564-3596

■ **Louisiana**
Bennie J. Fontenot, Jr.
Administrator, Inland Fisheries
Division
LA Dept. of Wildlife & Fisheries
P.O. Box 98000
Baton Rouge, LA 70898-9000
504-765-2330
John Roussel
Administrator, Marine
Fisheries Division
LA Dept. of Wildlife & Fisheries
P.O. Box 98000
Baton Rouge, LA 70898-9000
504-765-2384

■ **Maine**
Peter M. Bourque
Director, Division of Fisheries
ME Dept. of Inland Fisheries &
Wildlife
284 State St., Station #41
Augusta, ME 04333
207-287-2871
Robin Alden
Commissioner
ME Dept. of Marine Resources
State House Station 21
Augusta, ME 04333
207-624-6550

■ **Maryland**
W. Pete Jensen
Director, Fisheries Division
Tidewater Administration
MD Dept. of Natural Resources
Tawes State Office Bldg.
Annapolis, MD 21401
410-974-3558

■ **Massachusetts**
Dr. Mark S. Tisa
Assistant Director
Division of Fish & Wildlife
Field Headquarters
One Rabbit Hill Rd.
Westborough, MA 01581
508-792-7270
Philip G. Coates
Director, Division of Marine
Fisheries
Leverett Saltonstall
State Office Bldg.
100 Cambridge St.
Boston, MA 02202
617-727-3193

Michigan

John M. Robertson
Chief, Fisheries Division
MI Dept. Natural Resources
Box 30446
Lansing, MI 48909
517-373-1280

Minnestoa

Jack Skrypeck
Chief, Fisheries Section
MN Dept. Natural Resources
500 Lafayette Rd.
St. Paul, MN 55155-4012
612-296-3325

Mississippi

Ron Garavelli
Chief of Fisheries
MS Dept. Wildlife, Fish & Parks
P.O. Box 451
Jackson, MS 39205-0451
(2906 Bldg.)
601-364-2202
Fred Deegan
Chief, Marine Fisheries
MS Bureau of Marine Fisheries
152 Gateway Dr.
Biloxi, MS 39531
601-385-5899

Missouri

James P. Fry
Chief, Fisheries Division
MO Dept. Conservation
P.O. Box 180
Jefferson City, MO 65102-0180
314-751-4115 or
1-800-334-6946

Montana

Larry G. Peterman, Administrator
Fisheries Division

Thurston Dotson, Hatchery
Bureau Chief
MT Dept. Fish, Wildlife & Parks
1420 East Sixth
Helena, MT 59620
406-444-2449

Nebraska

Don Gabelhouse
Chief of Fisheries
NE Game & Parks Commission
P.O. Box 30370
Lincoln, NE 68503-0370
(2200 North 33rd St.)
402-471-5515

Nevada

James Curran
Chief of Fisheries
NV Dept. of Wildlife
P.O. Box 10678
Reno, NV 89520-0020
702-688-1569

New Hampshire

Charles A. Bridge
Chief, Inland Fisheries Division
NH Fish & Game Dept.
2 Hazen Dr.
Concord, NH 03301
603-271-2501
John L. Nelson
Chief, Marine Fisheries Division
NH Fish & Game Dept.
225 Main St.
Durham, NH 03824
603-868-1095

New Jersey

Bruce A. Halgren
Adminstrator, Marine Fisheries
Administration
Division Fish, Game, & Wildlife
Station Plaza 5, CN 400

501 East State St.
Trenton, NJ 08625
609-292-2083
Robert Soldwedel
Chief, Bureau of Freshwater
Fisheries
Station Plaza 5, CN 400
501 East State St.
Trenton, NJ 08625
609-292-8642

■ **New Mexico**
Stephen E. Henry
Chief, Fish Management Division
NM Game & Fish Dept.
Villagra Bldg.
Santa Fe, NM 87503
505-827-7905

■ **New York**
Gerald Barnhart
Chief, Bureau of Fisheries
NY Dept. Environmental
Conservation
50 Wolf Rd., Room 552
Albany, NY 12233-4753
518-457-5420
Gordon Colvin
Director, Division of Marine
Resources
205 Belle Meade Ave.
E. Setauket, NY 11733
516-751-7900

■ **North Carolina**
Robert L. Curry
Program Manager, Boating & Inland
Fisheries
NC Wildlife Resources Commission
512 N. Salisbury St.
Raleigh, NC 27604-1188
919-733-3633
Bruce Freeman

Director, Division of Marine
Fisheries
NC Dept. Envn., Health, & Natural
Resources
P.O. Box 769
Morehead City, NC 28557-0769
919-726-7021 or
800-338-7806

■ **North Dakota**
Terry R. Steinwand
Chief, Fishery Division
ND Game & Fish Dept.
100 North Bismarck Expressway
Bismarck, ND 58501
701-328-6313

■ **Ohio**
Gary Isbelle
Executive Administrator
Fish Management Research Group
OH Dept. Natural Resources
1840 Belcher Dr.
Columbus, OH 43224
614-265-6300

■ **Oklahoma**
Kim E. Erickson
Chief, Fisheries Division
OK Dept. Wildlife Conservation
P.O. Box 53465
Oklahoma City, OK 73152
405-521-3721

■ **Oregon**
Douglas DeHart
Acting Assistant Director, Fisheries
OR Dept. of Fish & Wildlife
P.O. Box 59
Portland, OR 97201
503-229-5400

■ **Pennsylvania**
Delano R. Graff
Director, Bureau of Fisheries

PA Fish Commission
450 Robinson Lane
Bellefonte, PA 16823-9616
814-359-5154

Rhode Island
John Stolgitis
Chief, Division of Fish & Wildlife Dept.
Environmental Management Government Ctr.
4808 Tower Hill Rd.
Wakefield, RI 02879
401-789-3094

South Carolina
Val Nash
Chief, Freshwater Fisheries
Wildlife & Marine Resources Dept.
Rembert C. Dennis Bldg.
P.O. Box 167
Columbia, SC 29202
803-734-3886
Paul A. Sandifer
Director, Division of Marine Resources
Wildlife & Marine Resources Dept.
Box 12559
1217 Ft. Johnson Rd.
Charleston, SC 29422-2559
803-795-6350

South Dakota
Robert L. Hanten
Cheif of Fisheries
SD Game, Fish & Parks Dept.
523 East Capitol
Pierre, SD 57501-3182
605-773-3384

Tennessee
C. Wayne Pollock
Chief, Fish Management Division
TN Wildlife Resources Agency

P.O. Box 40747
Nashville, TN 37204
615-781-6575

Texas
Gene McCarty
Division Director Coastal Fisheries
TX Parks & Wildlife Dept.
4200 Smith School Rd.
Austin, TX 78744
Phillip Durocher
Division Director Inland Fisheries
TX Parks & Wildlife Dept.
4200 Smith School Rd.
Austin, TX 78744
512-389-4862

Utah
Randy Radant
Chief, Fisheries Management
UT Division of Wildlife Resources
1596 West North Temple
Salt Lake City, UT 84116-3154
801-538-4700

Vermont
Tim Hess
Director of Fisheries
VT Dept. Fish & Wildlife
Waterbury Complex - 10 South
103 S. Main St.
Waterbury, VT 05676
802-241-3700

■ **Virginia**
Gary Martel
Chief, Fisheries Division
VA Dept. Game & Inland Fisheries
P.O. Box 11704
Richmond, VA 23230-1104
804-367-0509
Jack G. Travelstead
Chief, Fisheries Management
Division
VA Marine Resources Commission
P.O. Box 756
Newport News, VA 23607
804-247-2200

■ **Washington**
Robert Turner
Director
WA State Dept. of Fish and Wildlife
600 N. Capitol Way
Olympia, WA 98501-1091
360-902-2200

■ **West Virginia**
Bernard Dowler
Chief, Wildlife Resources Section
WV Division Natural Resources
1900 Kanawha Blvd., East
Bldg. 3, Room 812
Charleston, WV 25305
304-558-2771

■ **Wisconsin**
Lee Kernen
Director, Bureau of Fish
Management
WI Dept. Natural Resources
Box 7921
Madison, WI 53707
608-267-0796

■ **Wyoming**
Stephen Facciani
Chief, Fish Division
WY Game & Fish Dept.
5400 Bishop Blvd.
Cheyenne, WY 82006
307-777-4559

Good things come in small packages.

The *Southern Living Cabin Collection* —
16 cabin and cottage designs for country living

Find the perfect weekend cabin, guest house, or year-round country cottage in the *Southern Living Cabin Collection*. Ranging in size from 680 to 1,800 square feet, these 16 plans are thrifty on space but don't stint on comfort. The *Cabin Collection* is designed by Bill Phillips, AIA, who is also the creator of the popular *Southern Living Cottage Collection*. Order today!

PB-1096-725; **$18**.

Just $18 plus shipping and handling.
Call 1-800-755-1122 for credit card orders.

ACKNOWLEDGMENTS

Special thanks...

to the following for sharing material: George Lewis, University of Georgia; John Jensen, Auburn University; Jim Davis and Dave Mayes, Texas A&M; Kenneth Williams, Langston University; Bill James, Indiana Division of Fish and Wildlife; and the Missouri Department of Conservation.

For additional copies of *Ponds: Building, Maintaining, Enjoying*, send a check or money order for $14.95 per book (including shipping and handling) to Ponds, *Progressive Farmer*, Box 830069, Birmingham, AL 35283-0069.